Mandala Drawing for Beginners

Learn How to Draw Mandalas
with Step-by-Step Tutorial

By Anna Quinn

Table of Contents

Disclaimer

While all attempts have been made to verify the information provided in this book, the author does assume any responsibility for errors, omissions, or contrary interpretations of the subject matter contained within. The information provided in this book is for educational and entertainment purposes only. The reader is responsible for his or her own actions and the author does not accept any responsibilities for any liabilities or damages, real or perceived, resulting from the use of this information.

The trademarks that are used are without any consent, and the publication of the trademark is without permission or backing by the trademark owner. All trademarks and brands within this book are for clarifying purposes only and are the owned by the owners themselves, not affiliated with this document. **

Introduction: What are Mandalas?

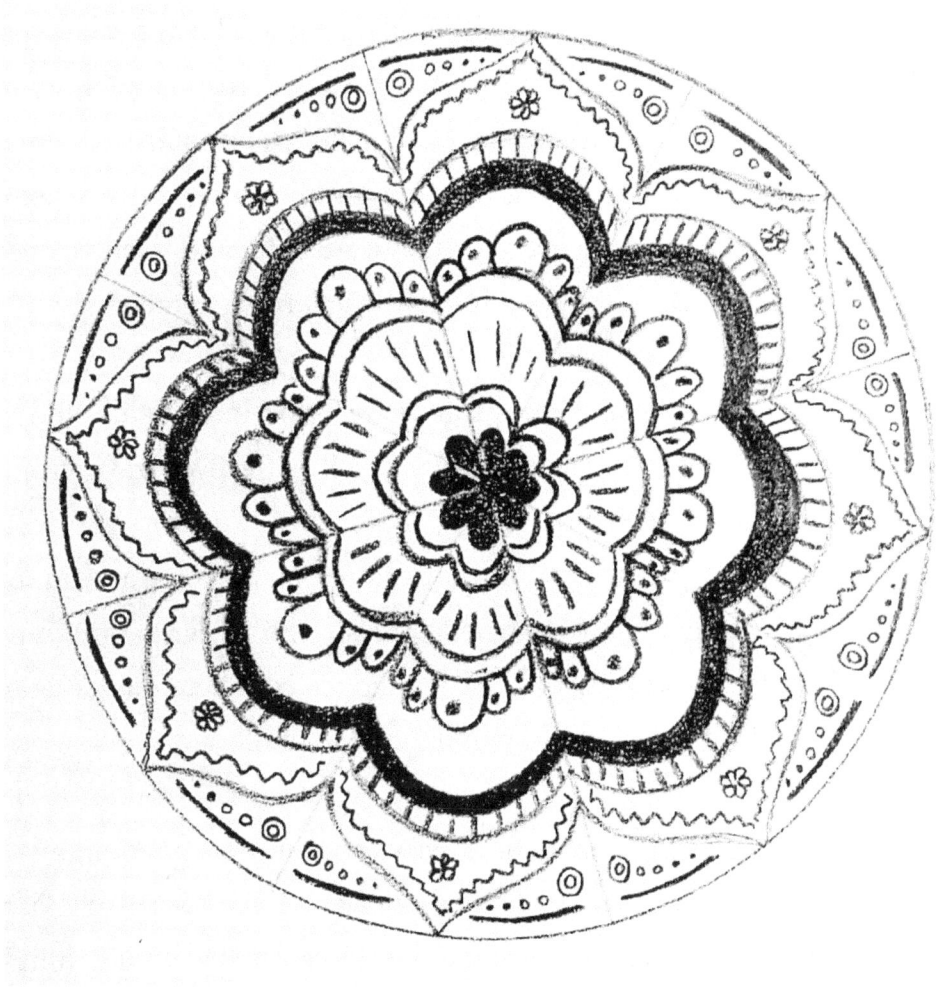

The word "mandala" is pronounced (mon-dah-lah), and its loosely interpreted meaning is "circle." In the world of art, mandalas are beautiful drawings that represent the universe and our infinite existence and wholeness as we relate to others. Mandala artwork has come to symbolize the balance and beauty of the universe, teaching us that all things come from the center core and reach outward to bring enlightenment to all life.

Years ago, Buddhist monks used mandalas as tools to help them focus during prayers and meditation. For them, the mandala was a sacred space where the spirit or deity resided in its center, opening the mind to spiritual thoughts as observers let their eyes and minds travel to the outermost parts of the circle. On their journey, those who studied the mandala gained balance, wisdom, and compassion. Along with their spiritual depths, mandalas are also thought to contain healing powers, where the artist can create with every mandala drawing a feeling of peaceful and positive energy that is passed to those who gaze upon its tightly balanced elements.

Whether the mandala contains mystical powers for individuals, few can resist being intrigued by its intricately woven spell as the eyes travel from its center and spiral to its outermost circle. Before you know it, you will be enjoying all the peace and relaxation that the mandalas offer as you learn how to create your individually designed pieces. The patterns on the page repeat themselves as do our lessons in life, and we complete one cycle only to begin another. That is the way of mandalas, and of life.

As you experiment with your mandalas, let your mind relax and allow your thoughts to carry you forward to faraway places or backward to old and favorite dreams. That's the fun of mandalas; they transport your mind to the best of all worlds—the one where mandalas reside.

Chapter 1: Drawing Your First Mandala

Soon you will be free-drawing mandalas, but, at first, we will draw them with structure until you get used to creating them with balanced repetition. In the following drawing, you will learn how to use space, size, and your center to form a beautiful mandala.

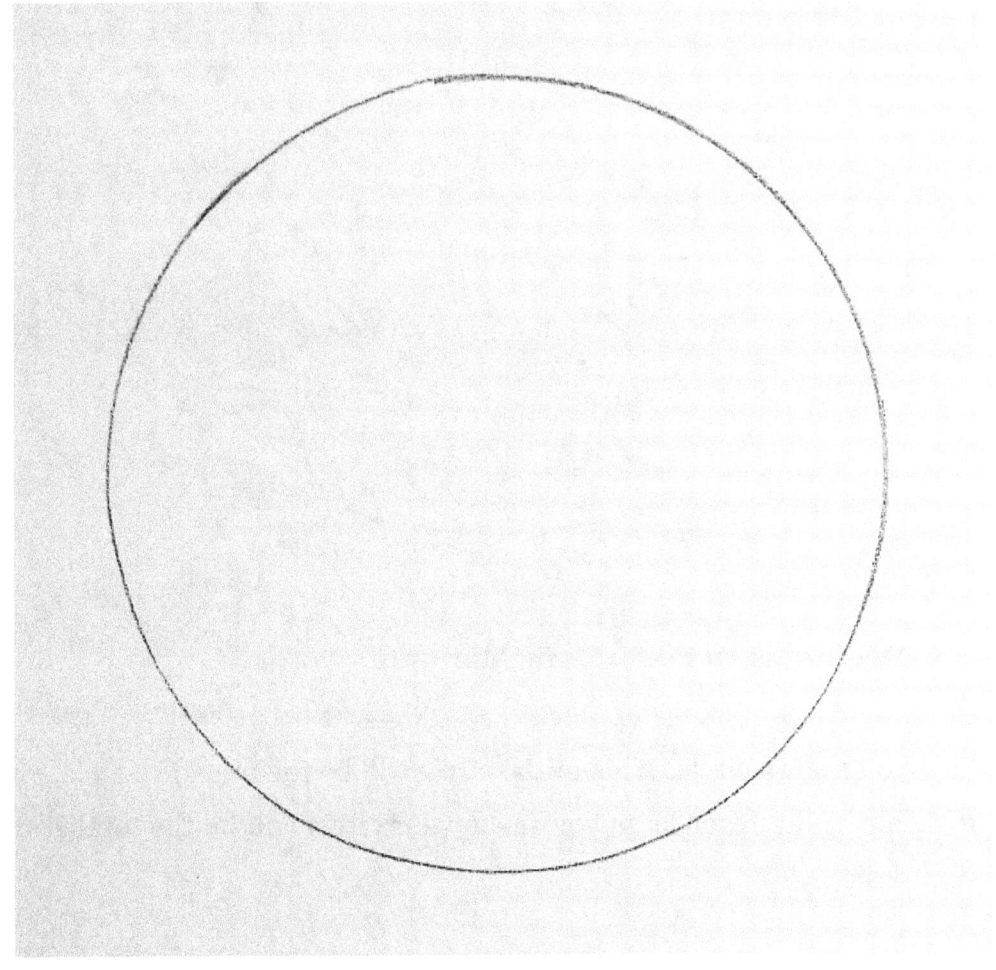

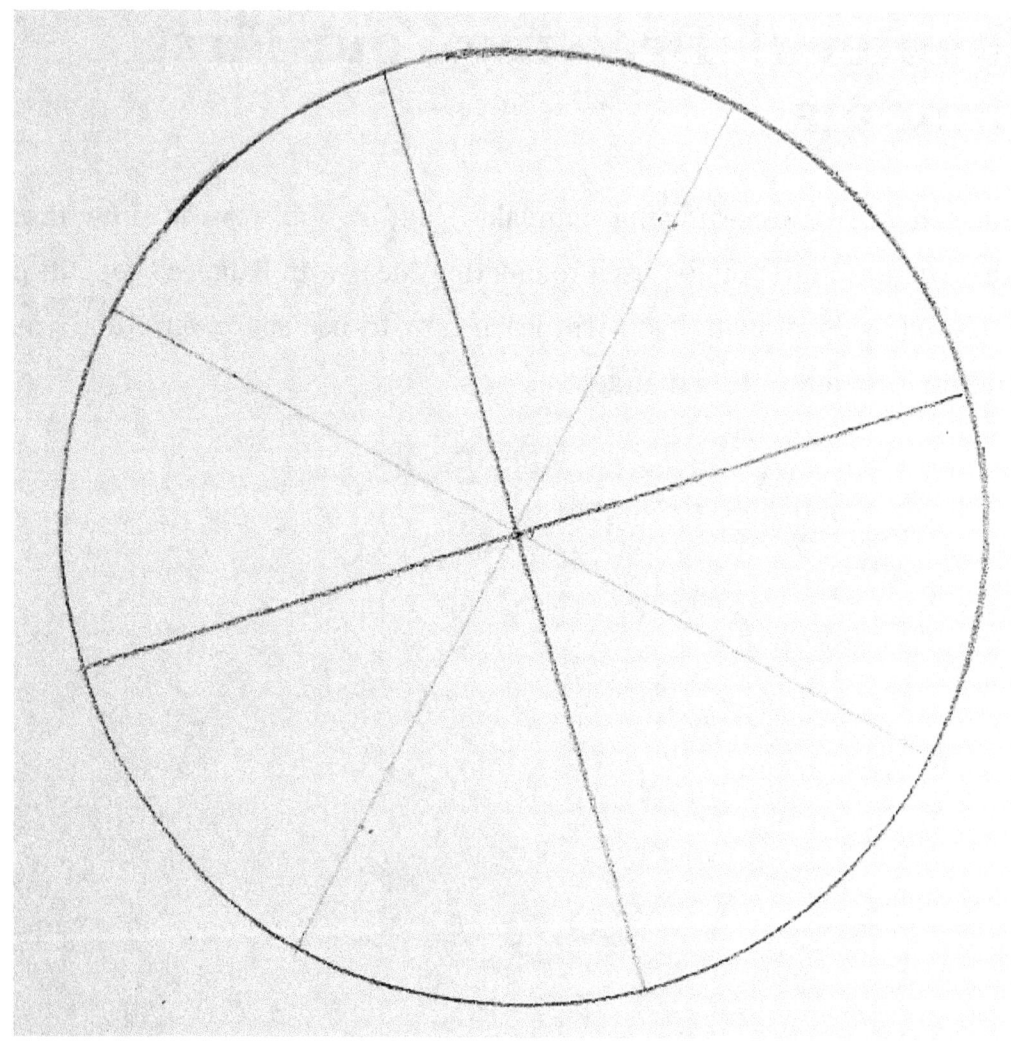

Step 1: Beginning to Form Your Mandala

- First you draw a circle. This initial circle will be the outside edge of your mandala, so however large you make your circle will be the total size of your design.

- The beauty about drawing mandalas is that you can use almost any medium you wish to sketch. Because you will be drawing many lines that you might sometimes drag your wrist across, it is preferable not to sketch with something that smears. You can use artist pens, colored pens, or any type of writing utensil that will help you to minimize unwanted smudges.

- Anything that can be used to draw a perfect circle is sufficient. One of the easiest ways to draw the circle is by using a protractor. However, there are times where it doesn't give you a large enough circle. Turning a large bowl upside down and drawing around it is fine as well. Just remember, this circle will make up the whole of your mandala.

Step 2: Dividing Your Mandala

- Now you can begin to divide your mandala into pie pieces.

- The easiest way to do this is to use a transparent ruler and divide your circle in half. Continue dividing the halves into halves until your circle has eight pie pieces.

- Notice that the first two lines are drawn darker than the others. This line will form your core or center point. As you divide these two lines in half again to create eight pie pieces, draw the lines lighter. You'll see why as we go along.

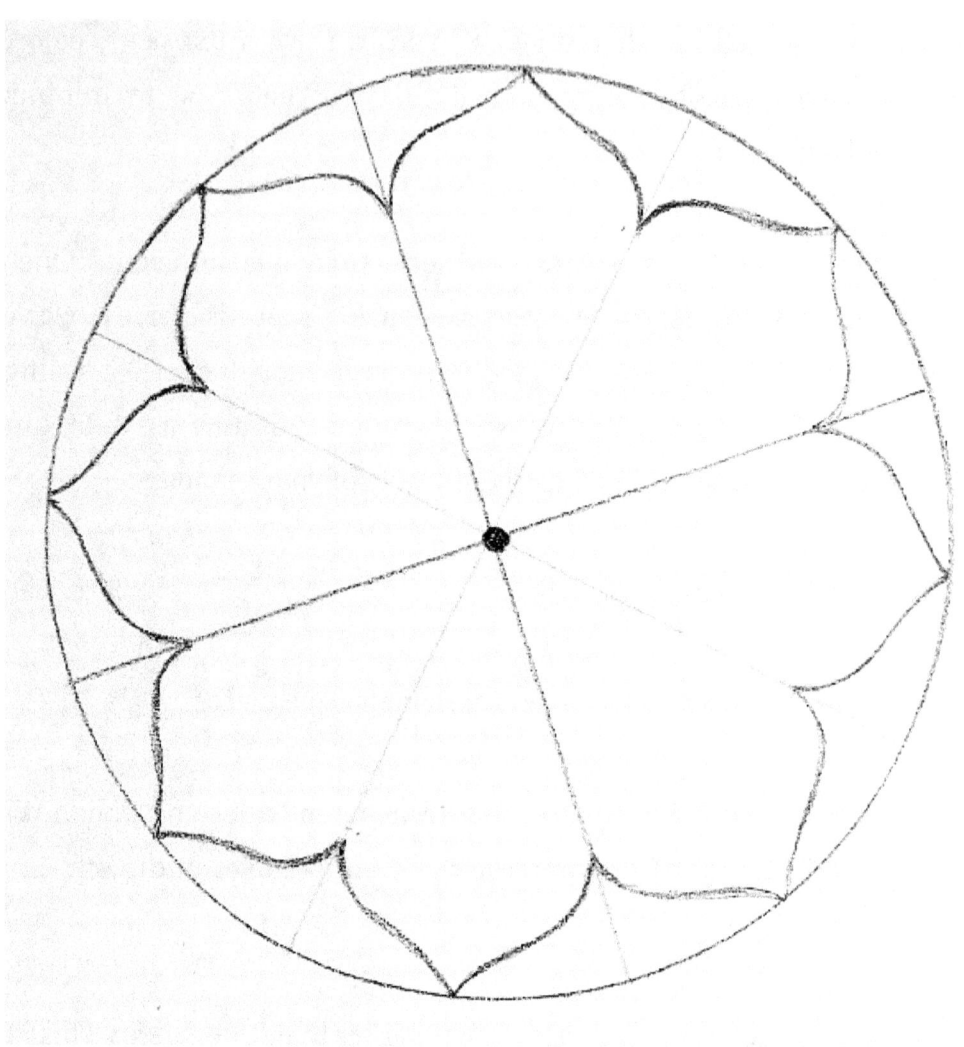

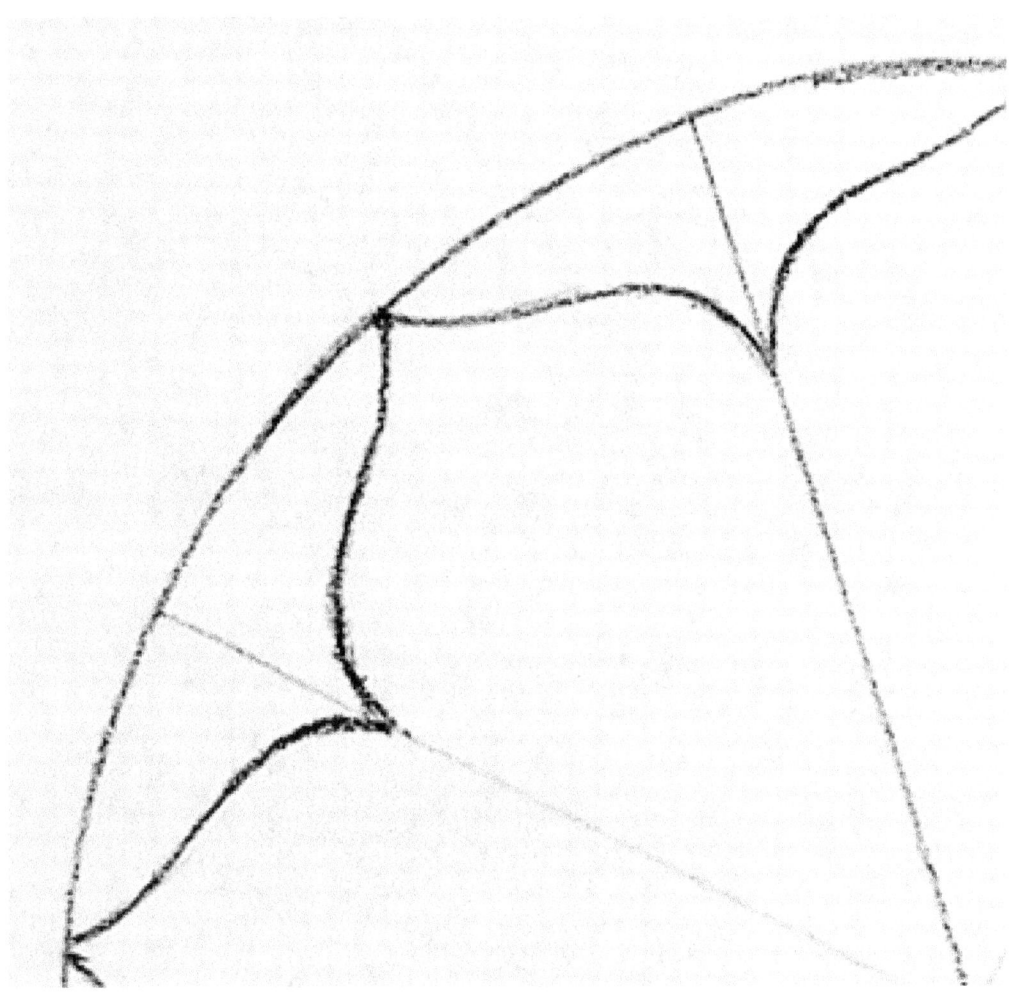

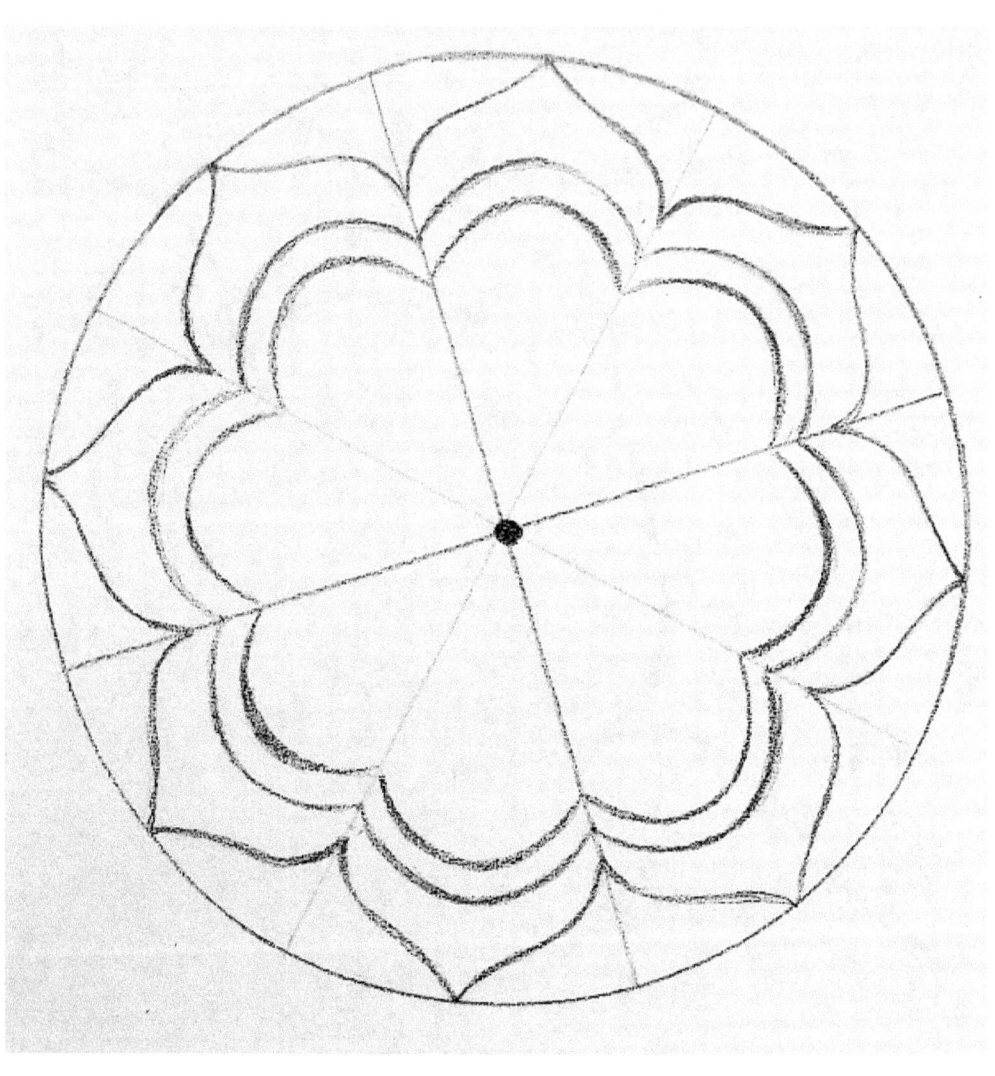

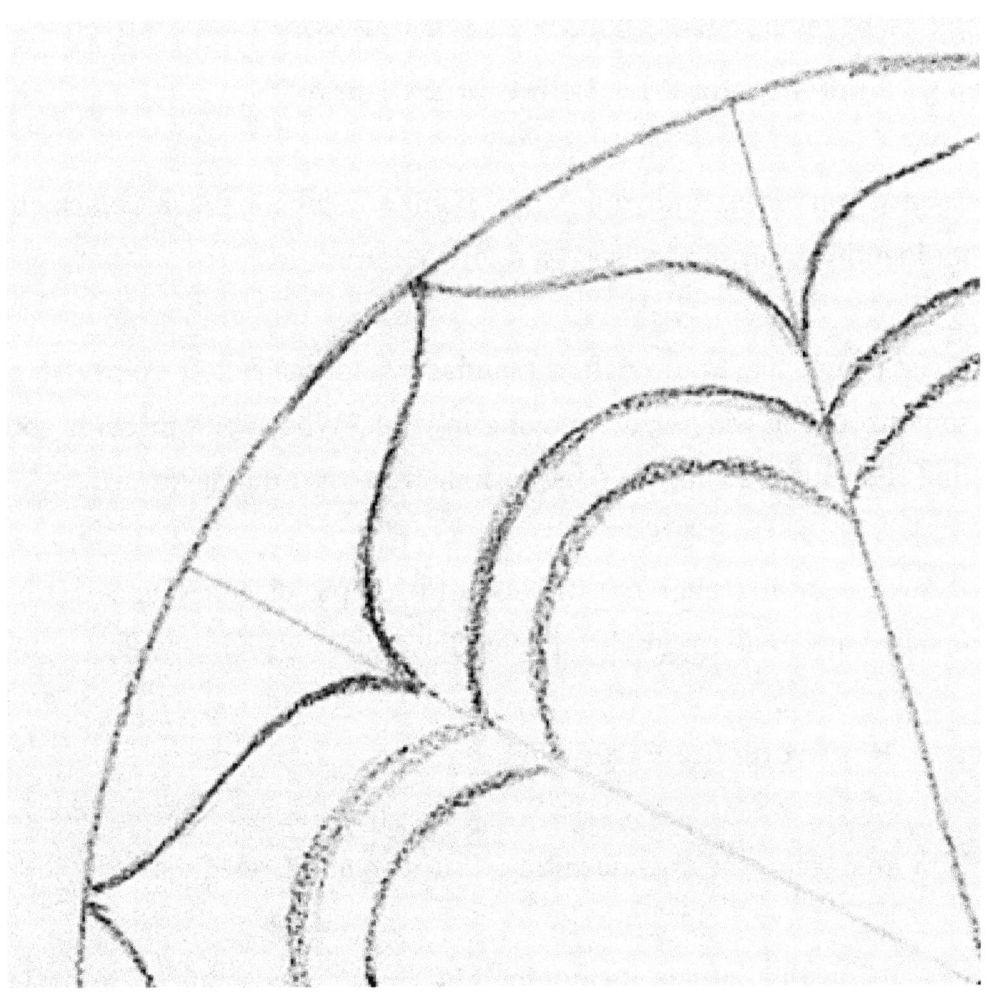

Step 3: Applying the First Pedals and Designs

- To give you focus, find your center point and create a small black circle for identification and to use as a reference point.

- Some people like to draw their mandalas from the center point out, and some from the widest part moving inward. Whatever works for you is fine. For this drawing, we'll be working from the outside inward.

- Draw a petal-like shape at the end of each pie piece. When you have finished, it should resemble an open flower.

Step 4: Repeating the Pattern

- Now, just below the outside petals, draw two half circled lines.

- Notice how the lines are beginning to draw your eyes inward toward the center of the circle.

- Make sure that your half circles touch to the sides of each pie piece.

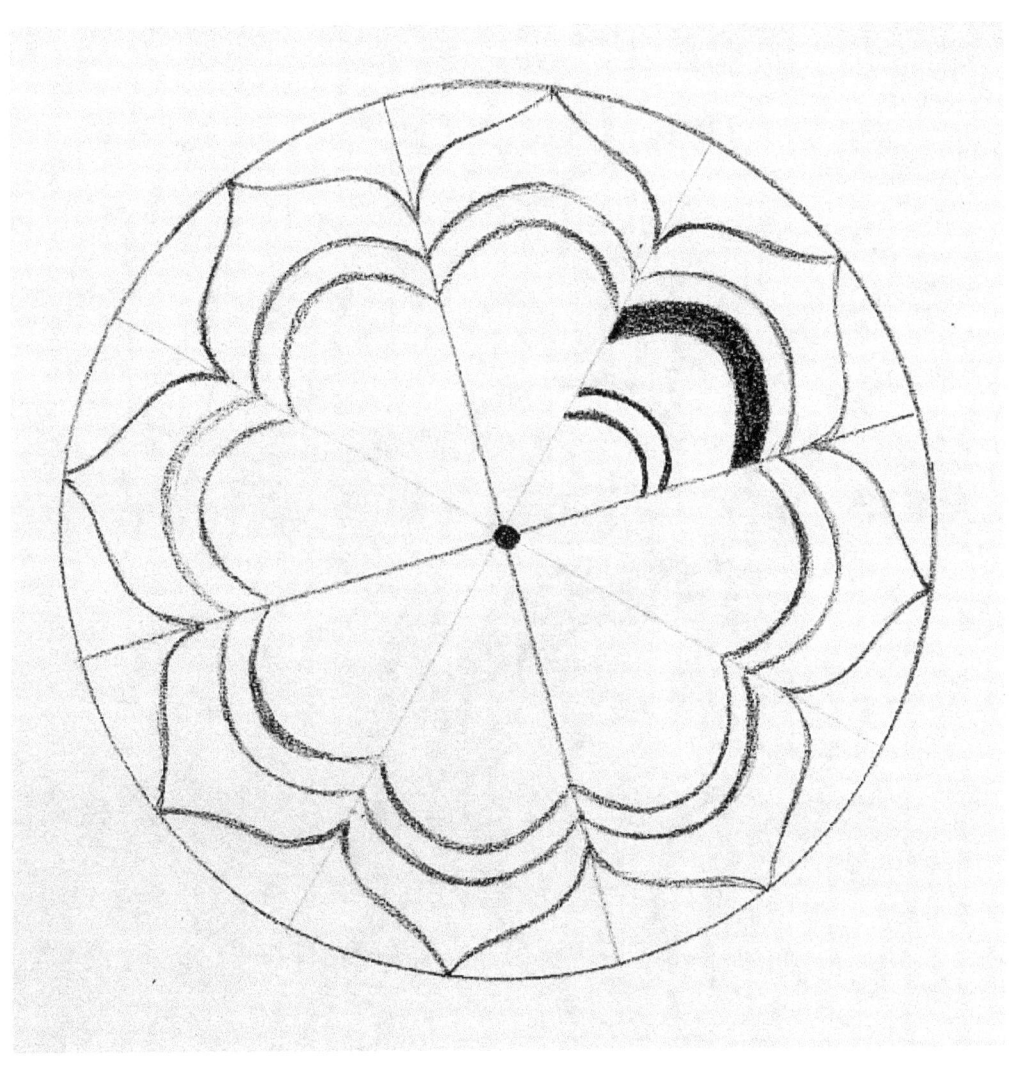

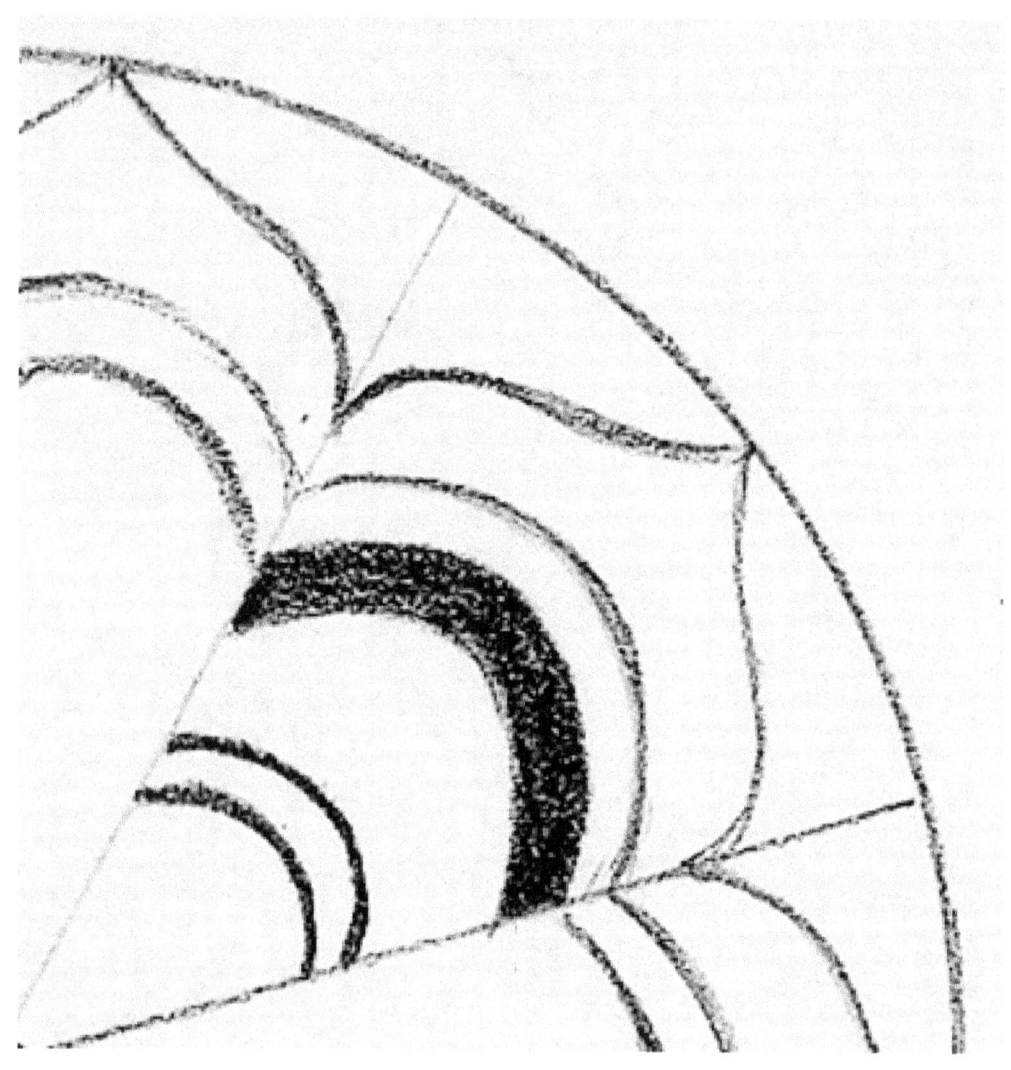

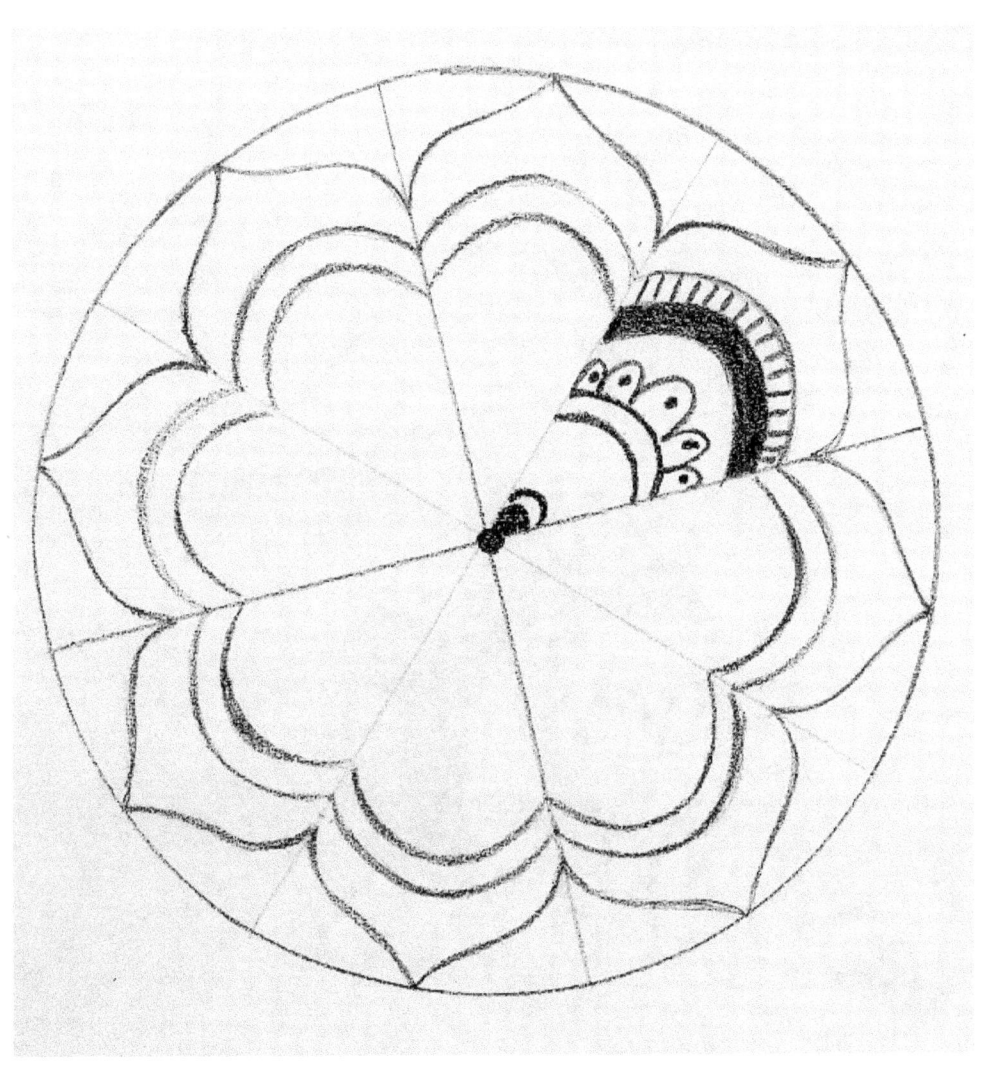

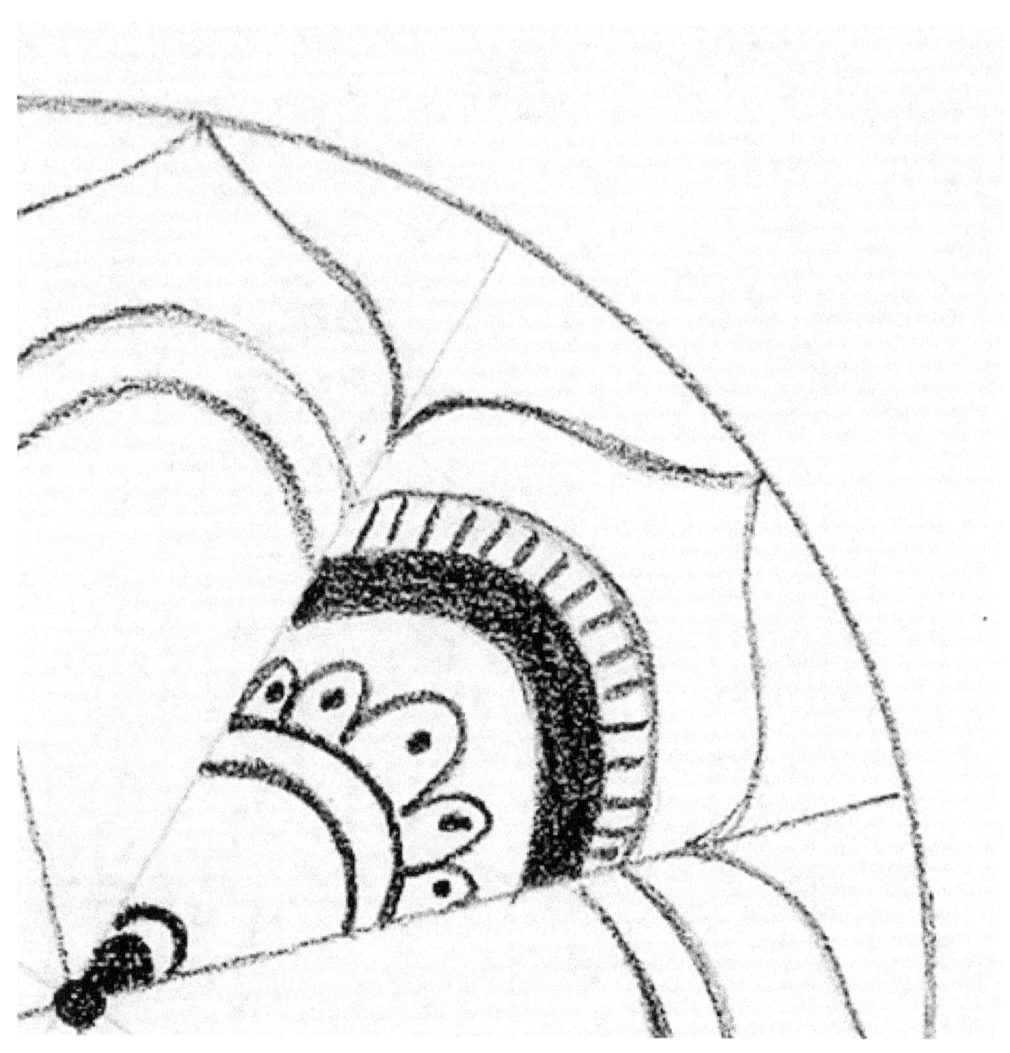

Step 5: Filling in the Spaces

- Working with only one pie piece, move just below the half circles you have drawn and draw another half circle.

- Be sure to make it approximately the same width as you did the first half circles.

- Now move down until you are about one-third from the center point and draw another two half circles, but only go as wide as the pie piece allows.

- Moving close to the center point, draw another two half circles.

Step 6: Filling in the White Spaces

- Draw vertical lines to look like tiny bars inside the top half circles in the pie piece.

- Fill in the space directly below that by darkening the ink in the space created by the next two half circles.

- Above the middle half circles, draw little loops that resemble daisy petals.

- Now, place a dot inside the wider end of the daisy petals.

- Notice how the daisy petals are smaller on the ends and gradually get larger as you move to the center petal. There should be five petals in all.

- As your eyes move to the center point, color in between the center dot and the close half circle. This should begin to resemble one petal of a small flower.

Step 7: Providing More Details in the White Spaces

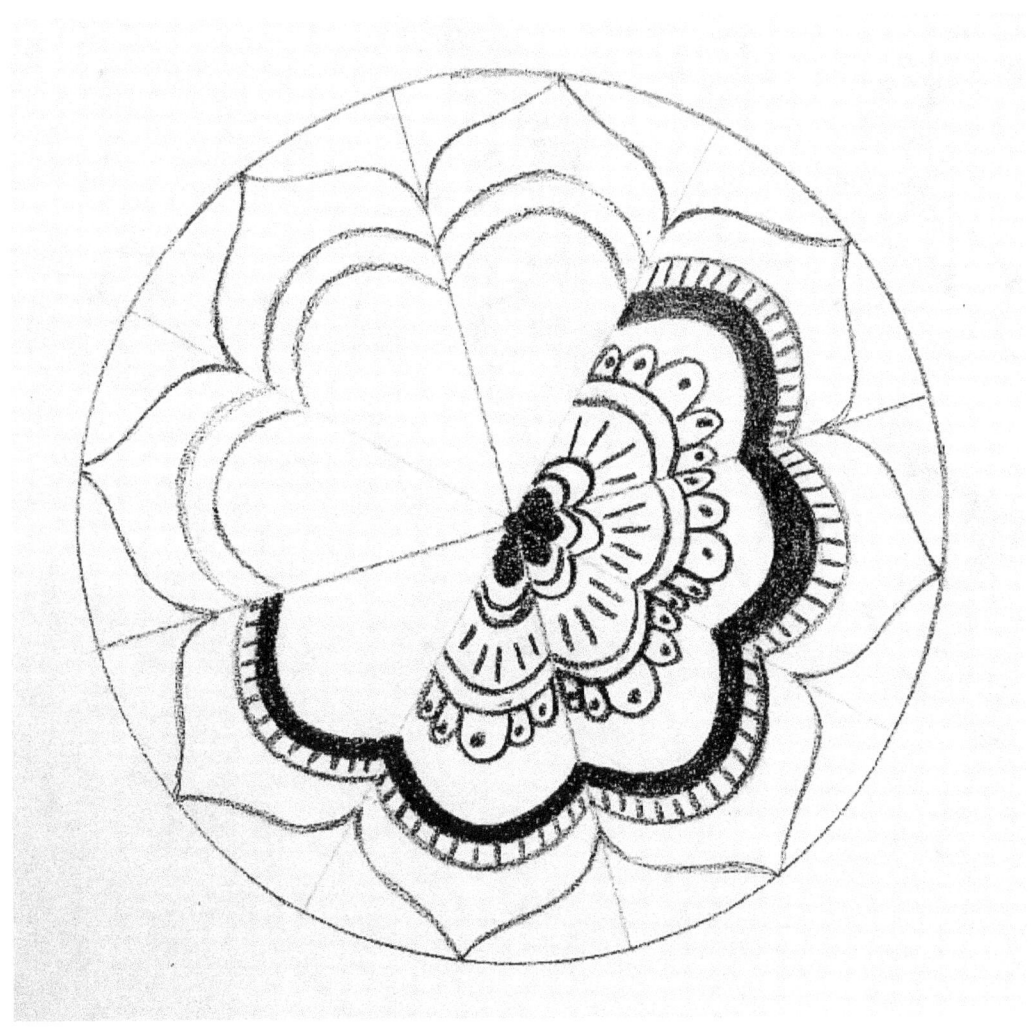

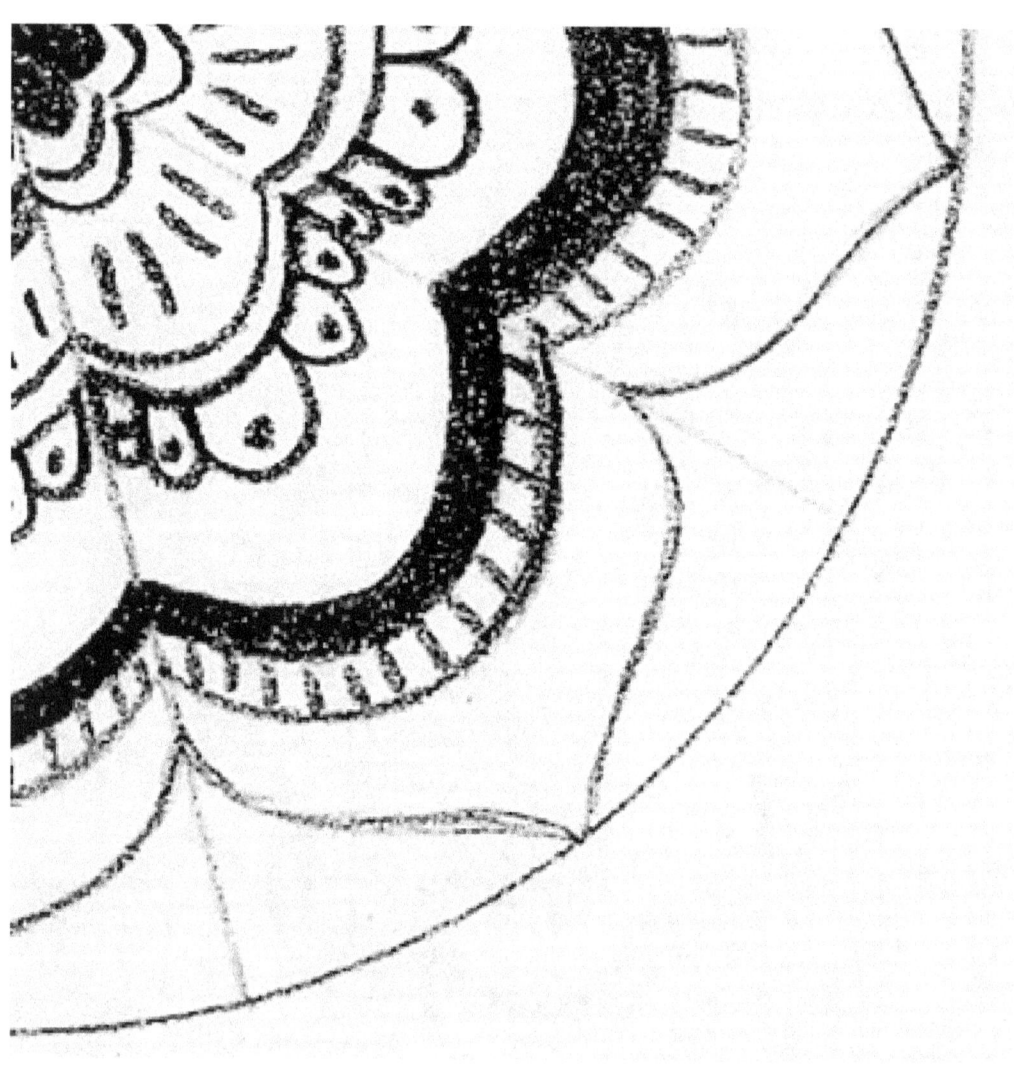

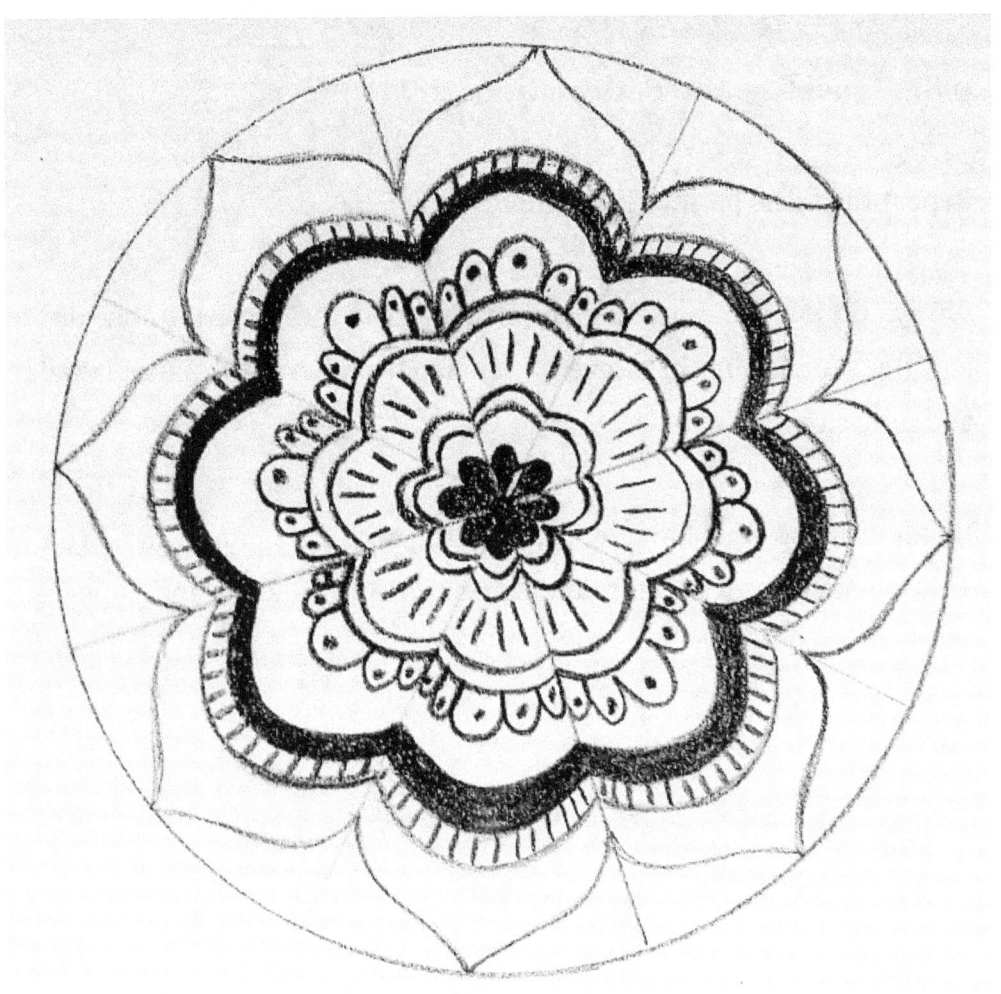

- Draw another half circle just above the one closest to the center point.

- Above the half, draw four lines that touch the top of the half circle and flare outward. Make sure they don't touch the bottom of the half circle just above them.

Step 8: Repeating the Pattern in Each Pie Piece

- Repeat the same pattern in each pie piece.

- Always do the same number of petal shapes, the same number of lines, and the same filling in of every pie shape to give your mandala balance and precision.

- When drawing your half circles, keep the spacing as uniform as you can. This will help to give your mandala proportion, balance, and appeal.

Step 9: Finishing Touches

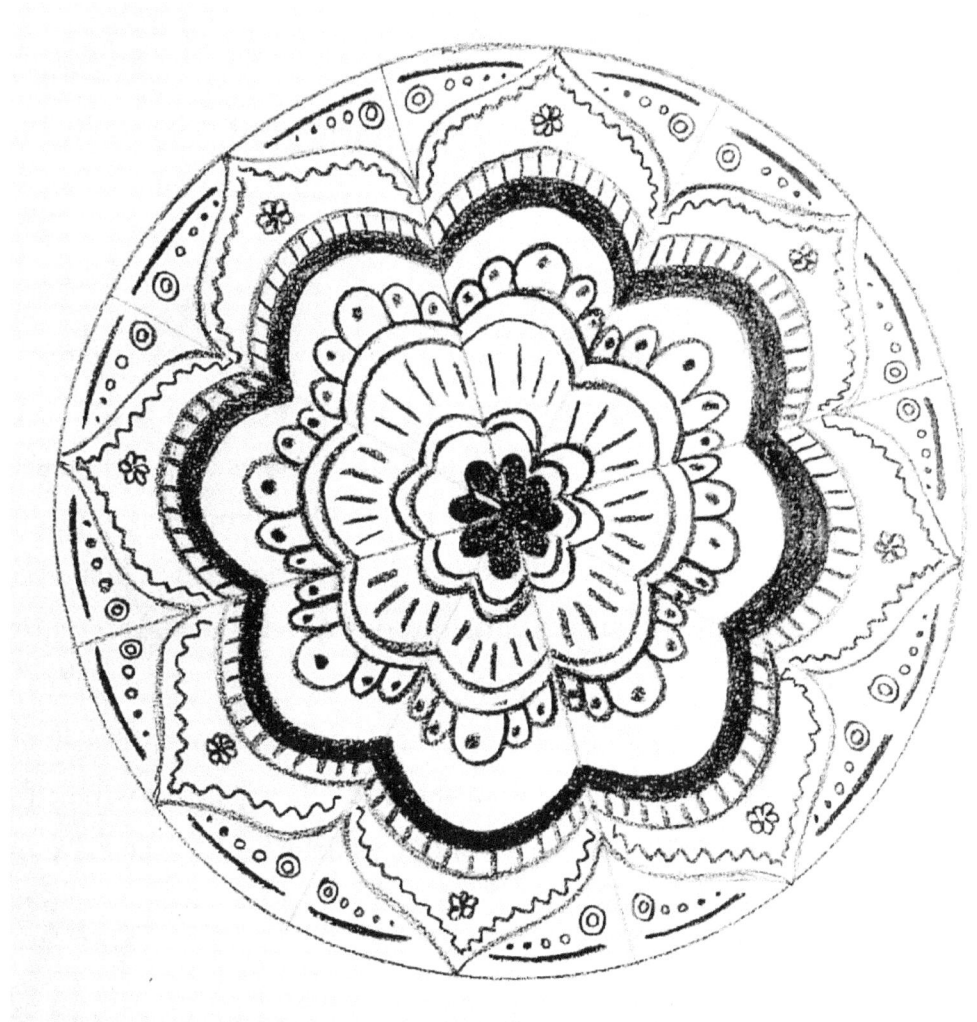

- Notice the finishing design touches. When you have finished filling in the pie pieces, you will begin to see white spaces that need some additional design. Don't be shy about filling in those spaces with special design work. However, make sure you add the same designs to each pie piece.

- Let's look at what was added to this mandala. On the inside of the largest outside petal, there is a wiggly line that moves around the petal like a little worm. It comes to a point at the petal's highest spot, and then follows the other side downward.

- At the inside point of each large petal is a small, five-petal daisy. You will see that it is just the hint of the daisy—without really giving each one a center point.

- On the outside of the large petals and just below the outside circle or lines, draw from the center of the petal point to the outside of the pie piece. Don't let the lines touch the petals or the edges of the pie pieces. When you have completed these lines, it should resemble large dashes. Make the space between these lines and the outside of the circle about the same width as the half circles you drew down each pie piece.

- Just below the dash line, draw five circles. The first three circles should be open, each one slightly larger than the next. The last two will just be solid dots. Make sure the largest open circles below the dashes face one another on the outside of each petal.

- Now, draw another circle around the largest open circle.

- Make sure you have repeated this pattern in all the pie pieces.

Step 10: Checking for Balance

- One of the most challenging things to do when drawing mandalas is to make them look symmetrically balanced.

- If your mandala looks out-of-balance, check your spacing and count your repeated designs. Make sure you haven't left any lines or petals out of any of the pie pieces. This will make it look off balanced.

- Now study the mandala for a few moments and enjoy its individual beauty and design repetition. Let your eyes flow from the inside out and the outside inward. Not only should you enjoy the design, but it should also make you feel pleasantly relaxed.

Chapter 2: Creating More Flow in Your Mandala

This mandala will have a softer, more free-flowing style.

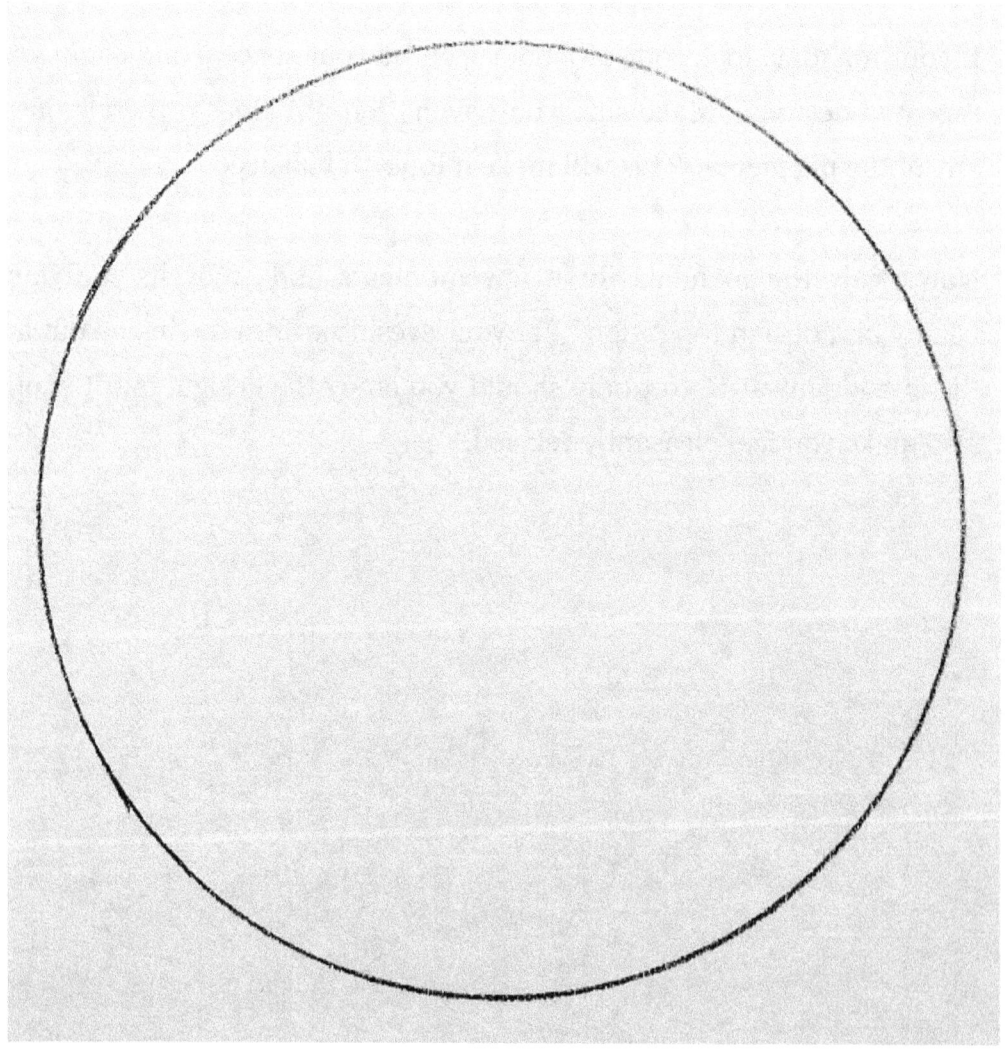

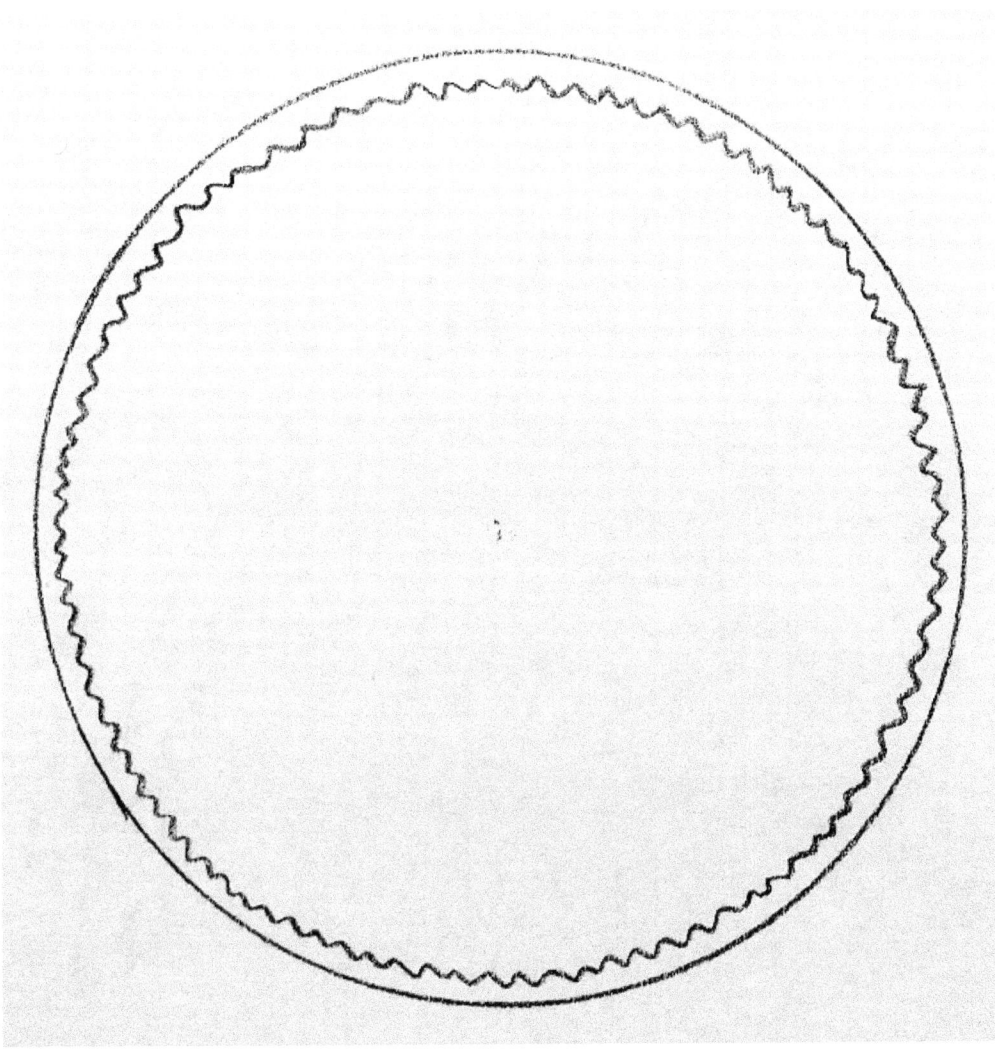

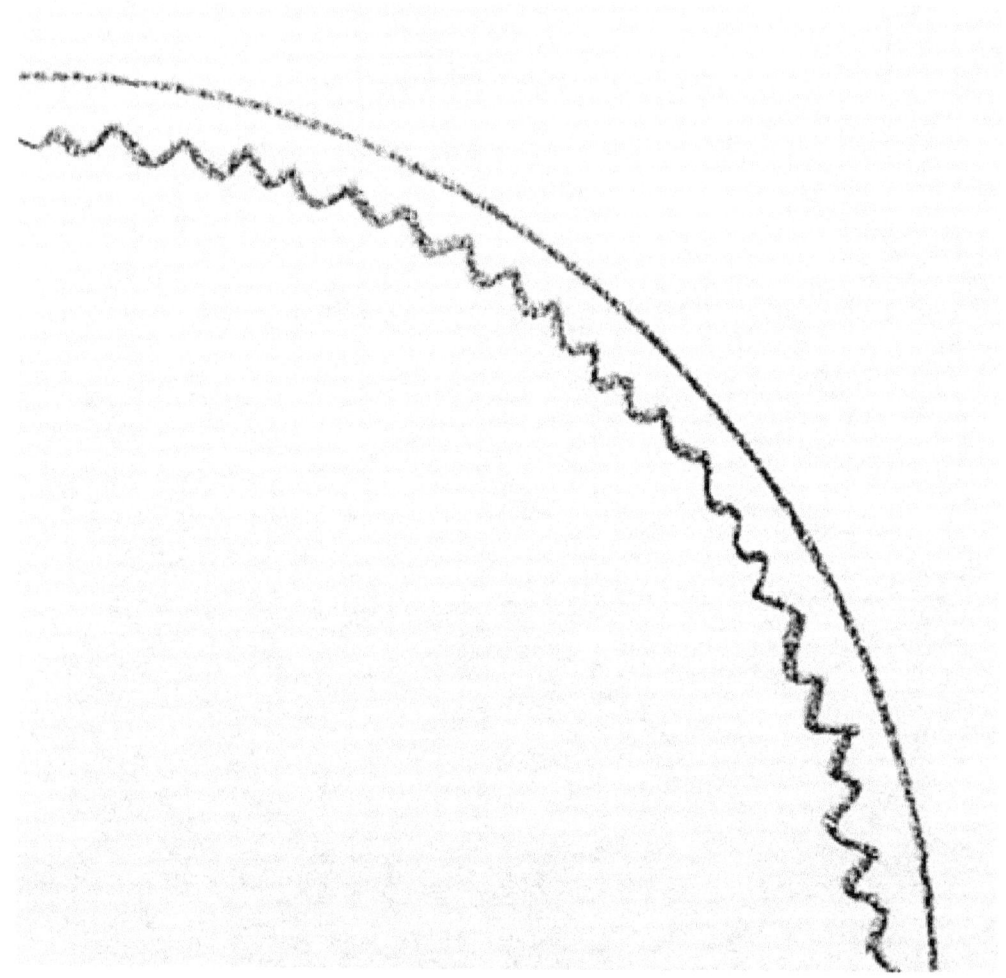

Step 1: Creating More White Space & Free-Flow

- Again, begin with the outside circle.

- Draw a wiggly line just inside your circle. This is drawn freehand.

Step 2: Drawing Your Inside Circles

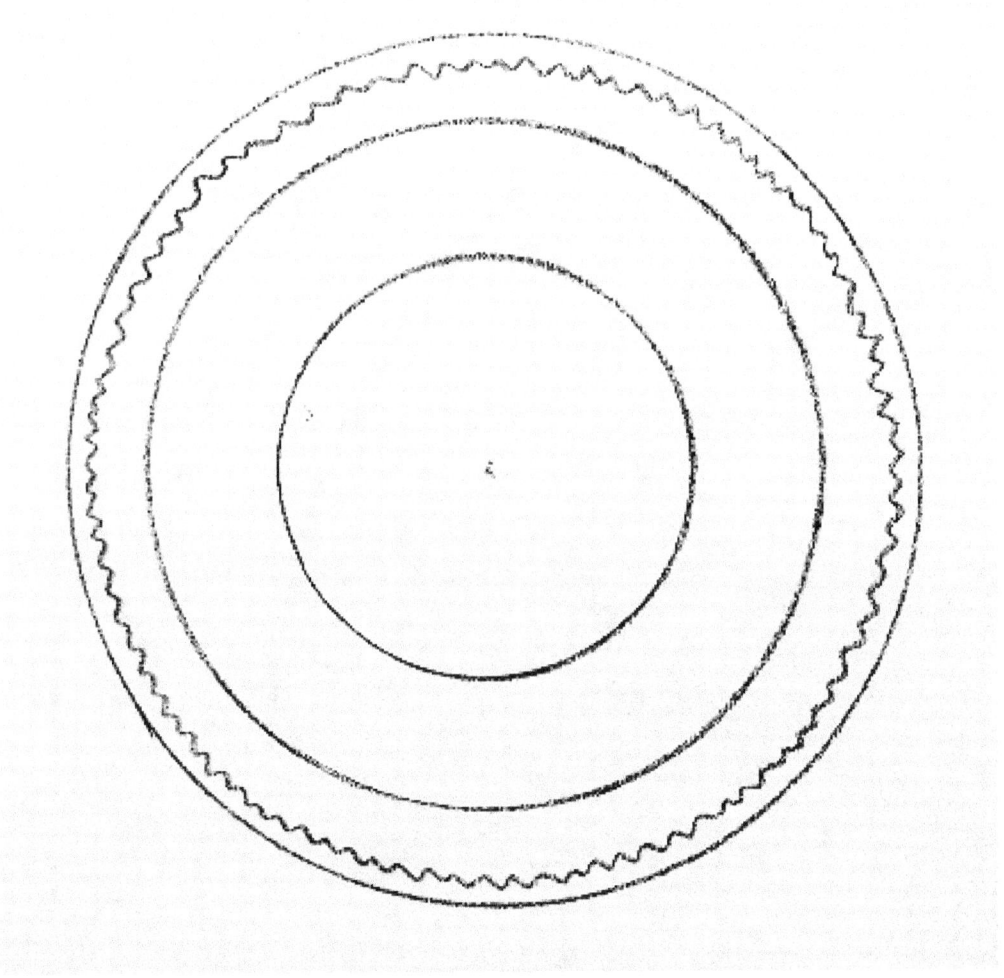

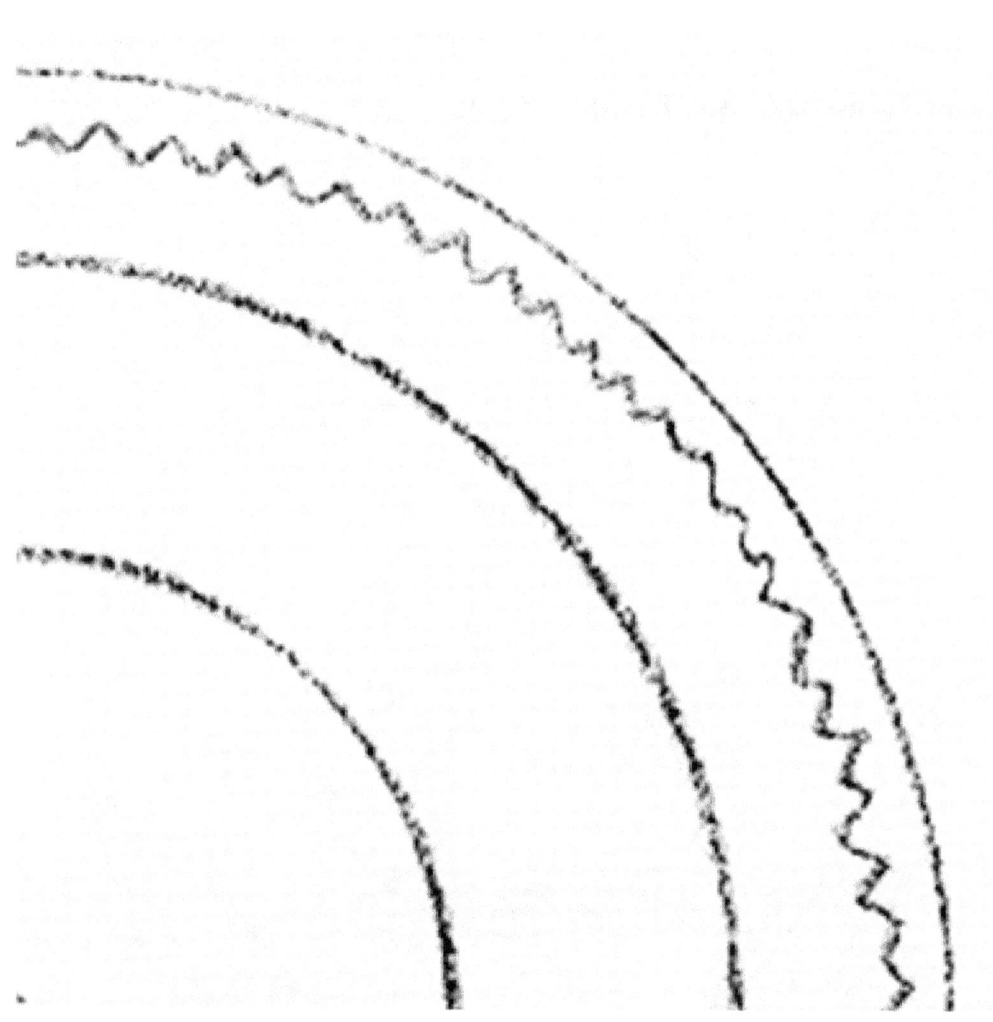

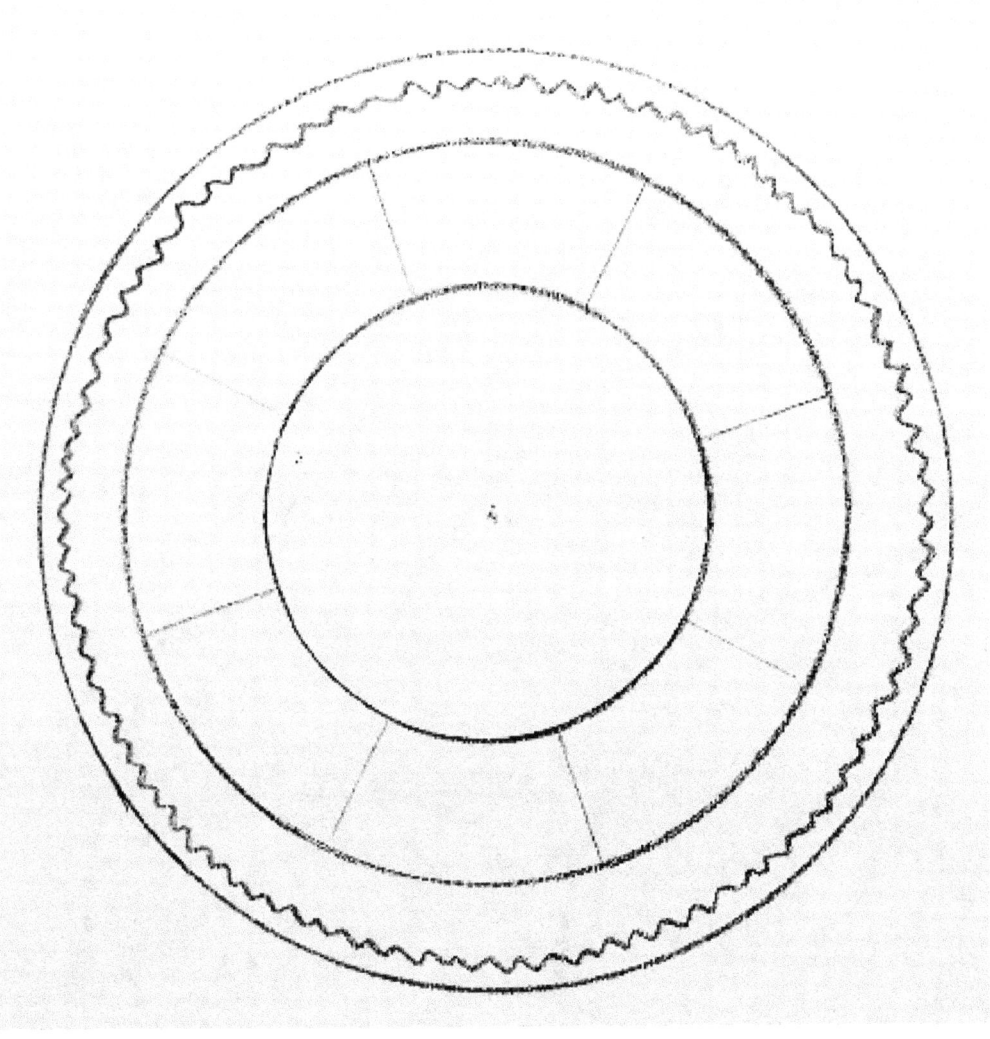

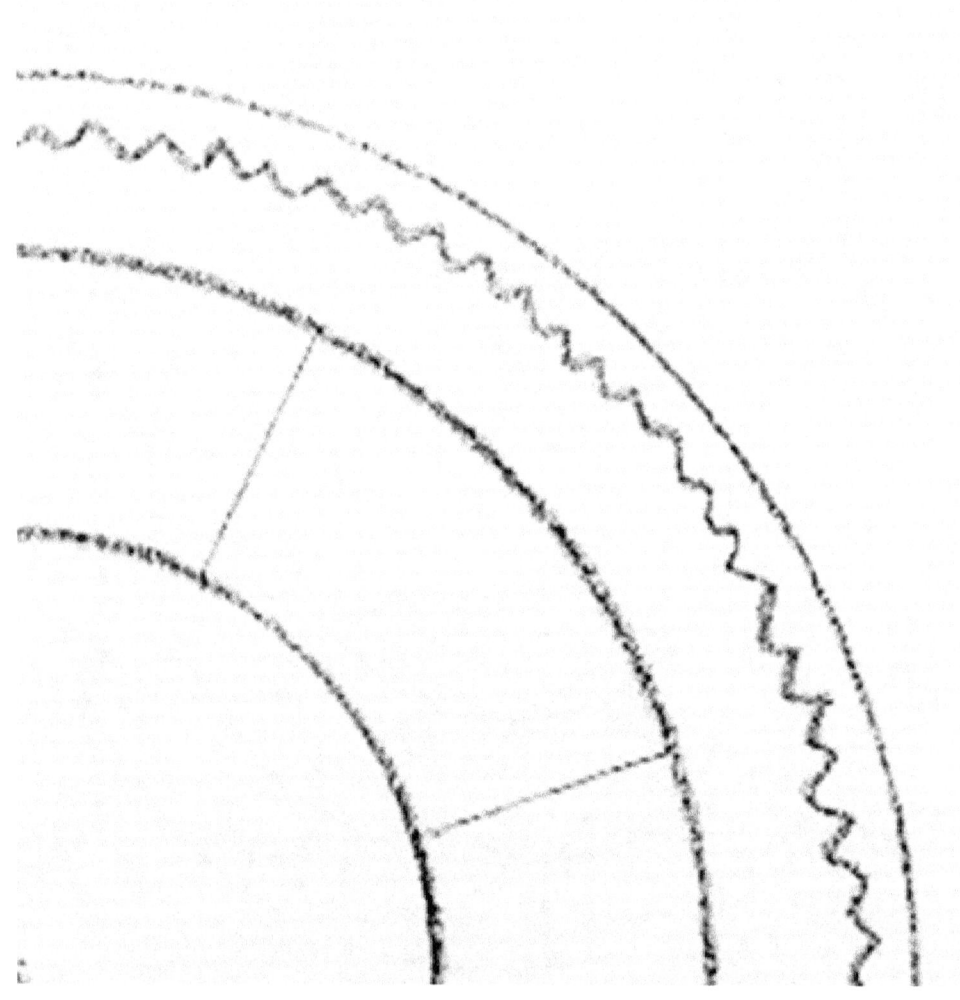

- You can either use three patterned circles, or a protractor for your circles.

- You'll need to draw two more circles inside your outside circle. One should be approximately one-quarter of the distance inside the outside circle. The other circle should be a little wider—just about halfway between your center point and the outside circle.

Step 3: Finding Your Center Point

- Just as you did in the first drawing, you're going to divide the circle into eight pie pieces. Only this time you will only mark the center point and the lines between your center and outside circles.

- You can use your transparent ruler to cross the center point as you did last time, only just draw the lines inside the middle circle—don't take it to the center point or to the outside circle.

Step 4: Adding the Leaf Pattern

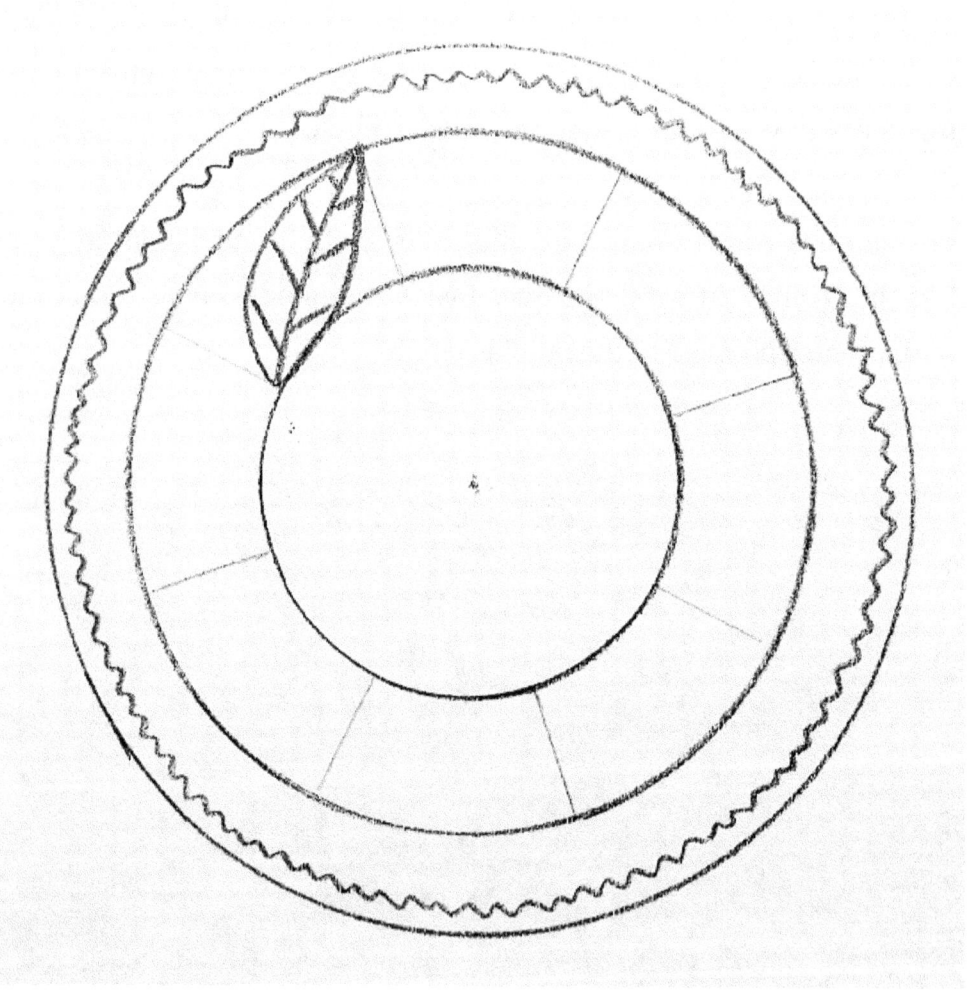

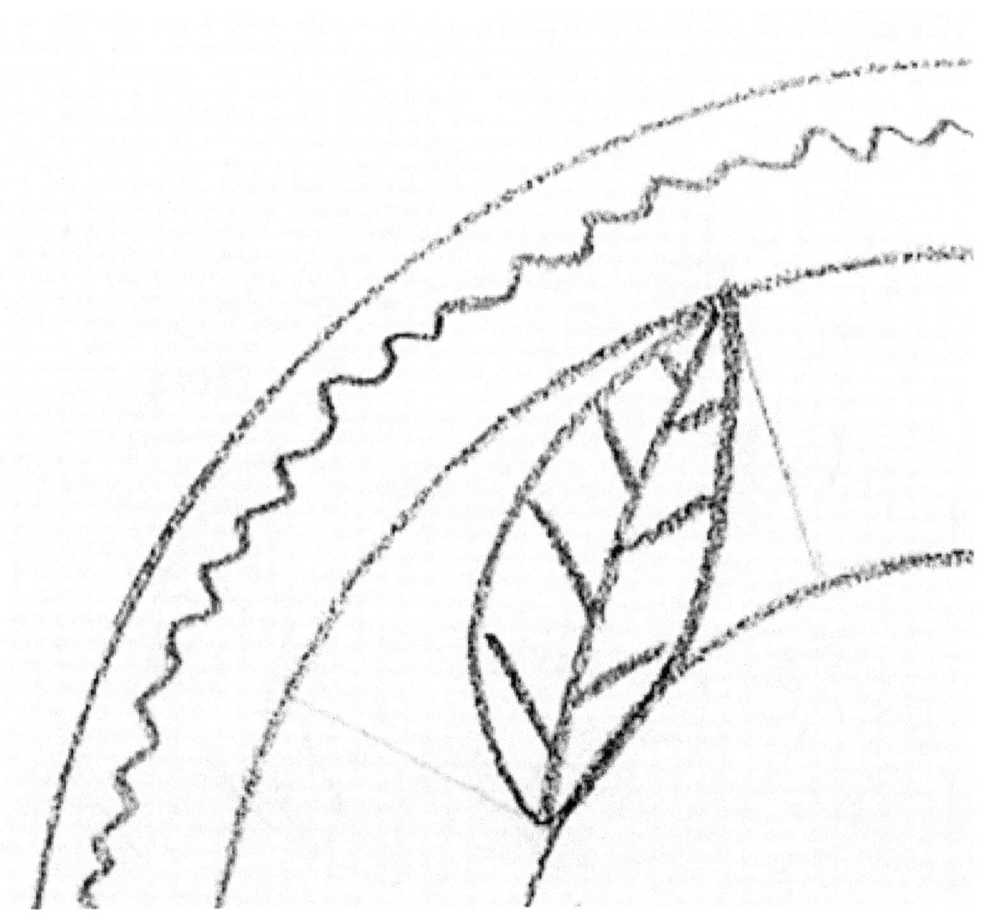

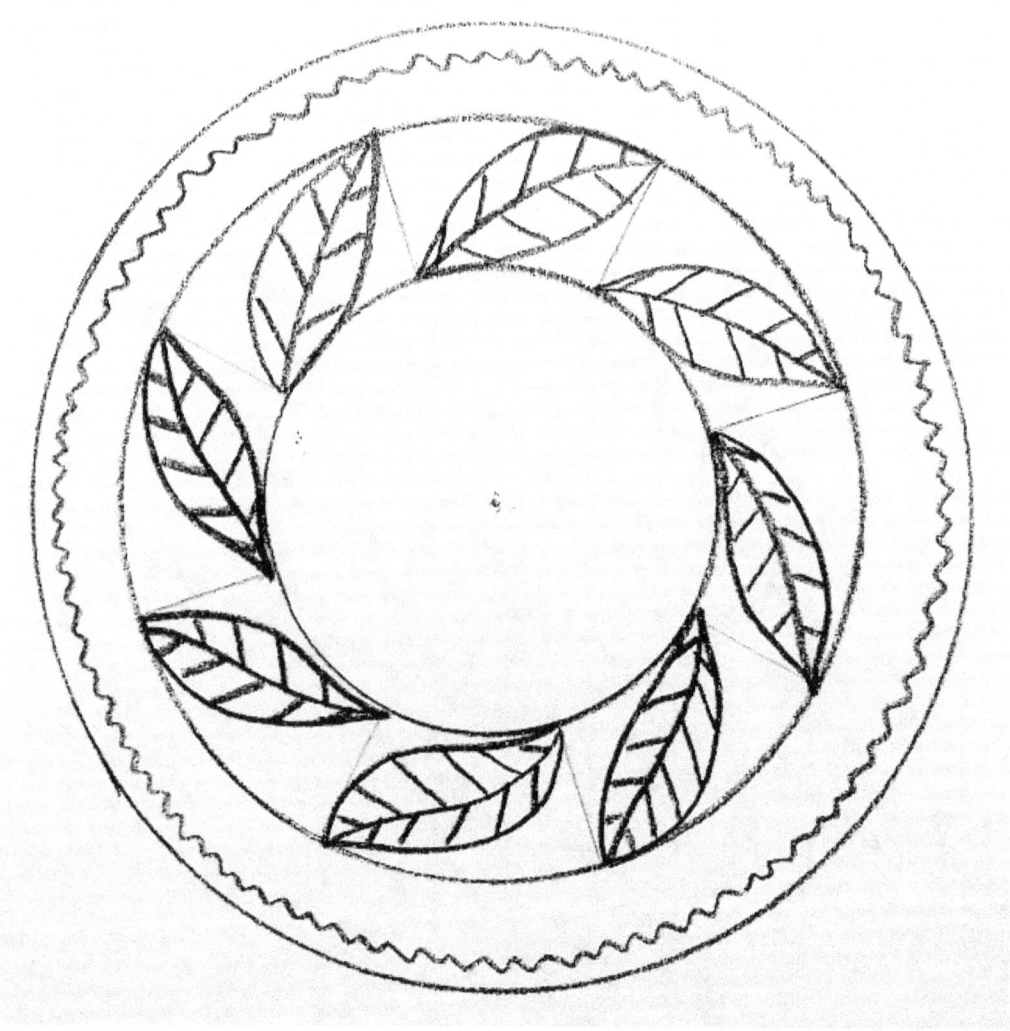

- Begin drawing the leafy pattern inside your eight small pie pieces.

- Draw the leaf diagonally, from the bottom left corner of the pie piece to the top right corner. Make sure all leaves are positioned in the same manner to give your mandala balance and proportion.

- Draw the center vein of the leaf, then four stems flowing from the center vein. Notice that the stems flowing from the center vein do not match up. Each one begins in the center of the next.

- The stems should touch from the vein to the outside of the leaf pattern. You might want to give the mandala more depth by making the leaves a bit darker than the rest.

Step 5: Adding details to the First Circle

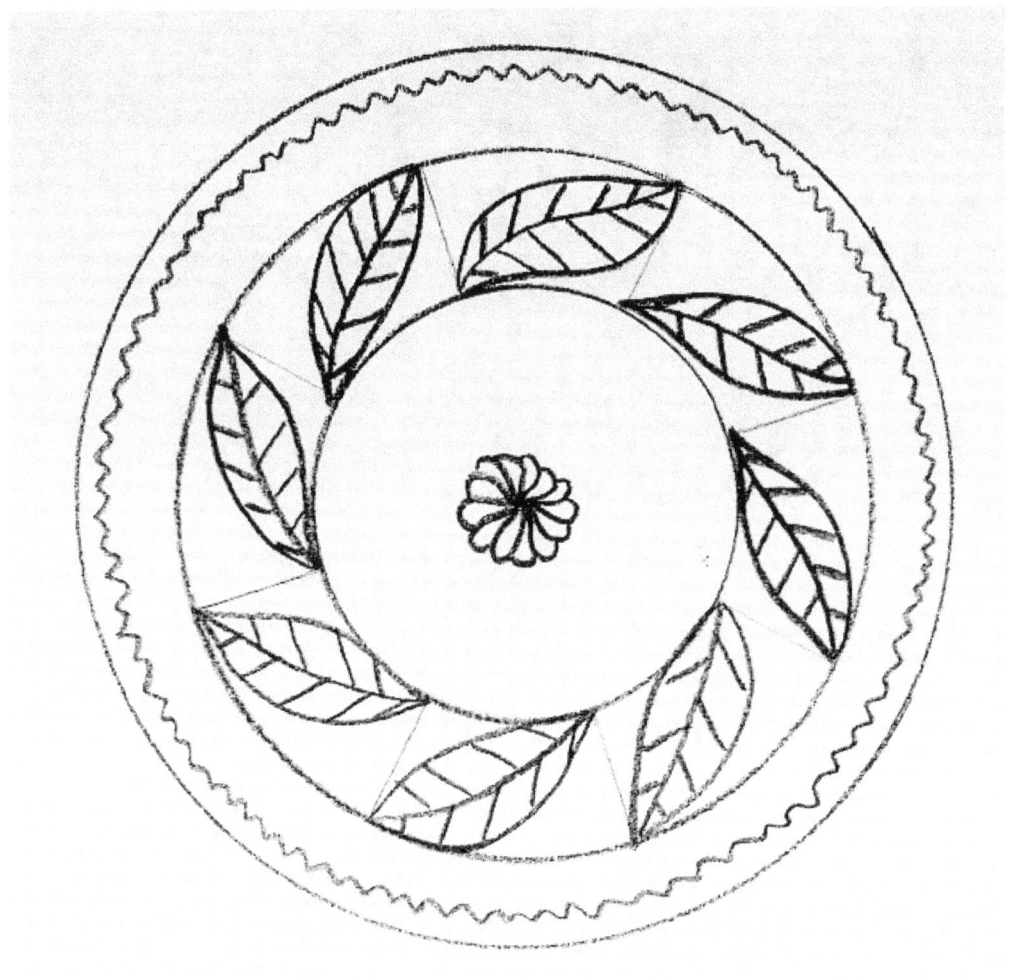

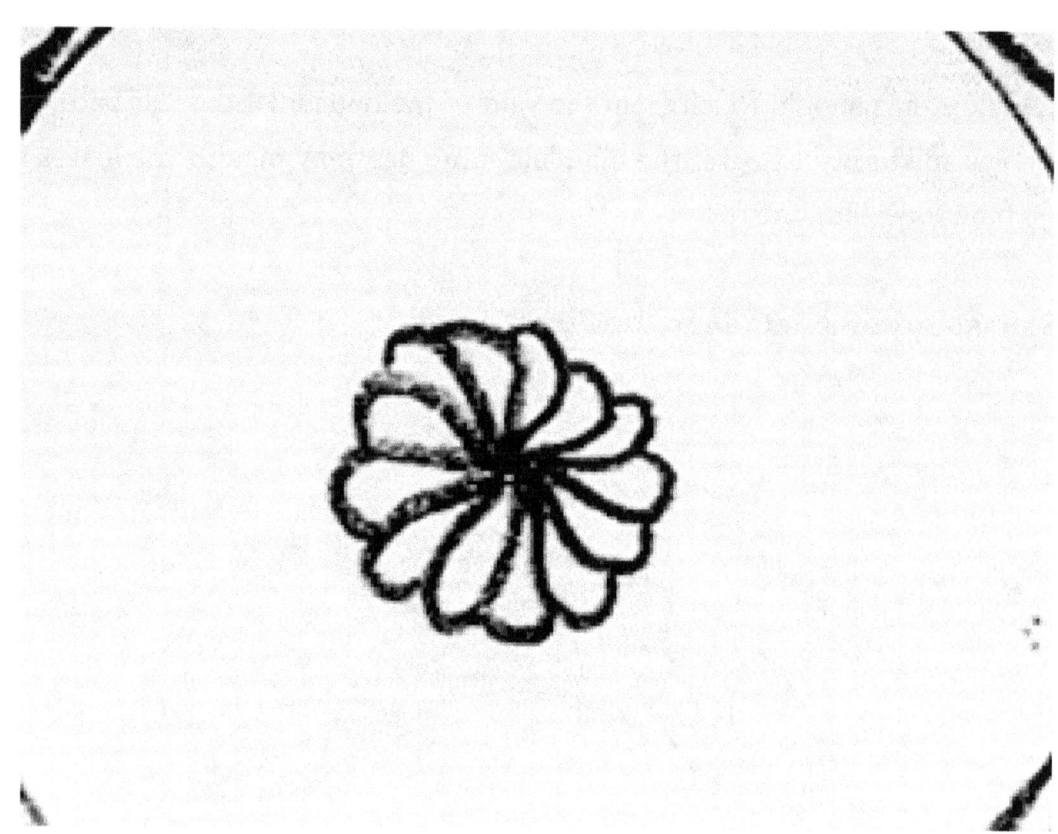

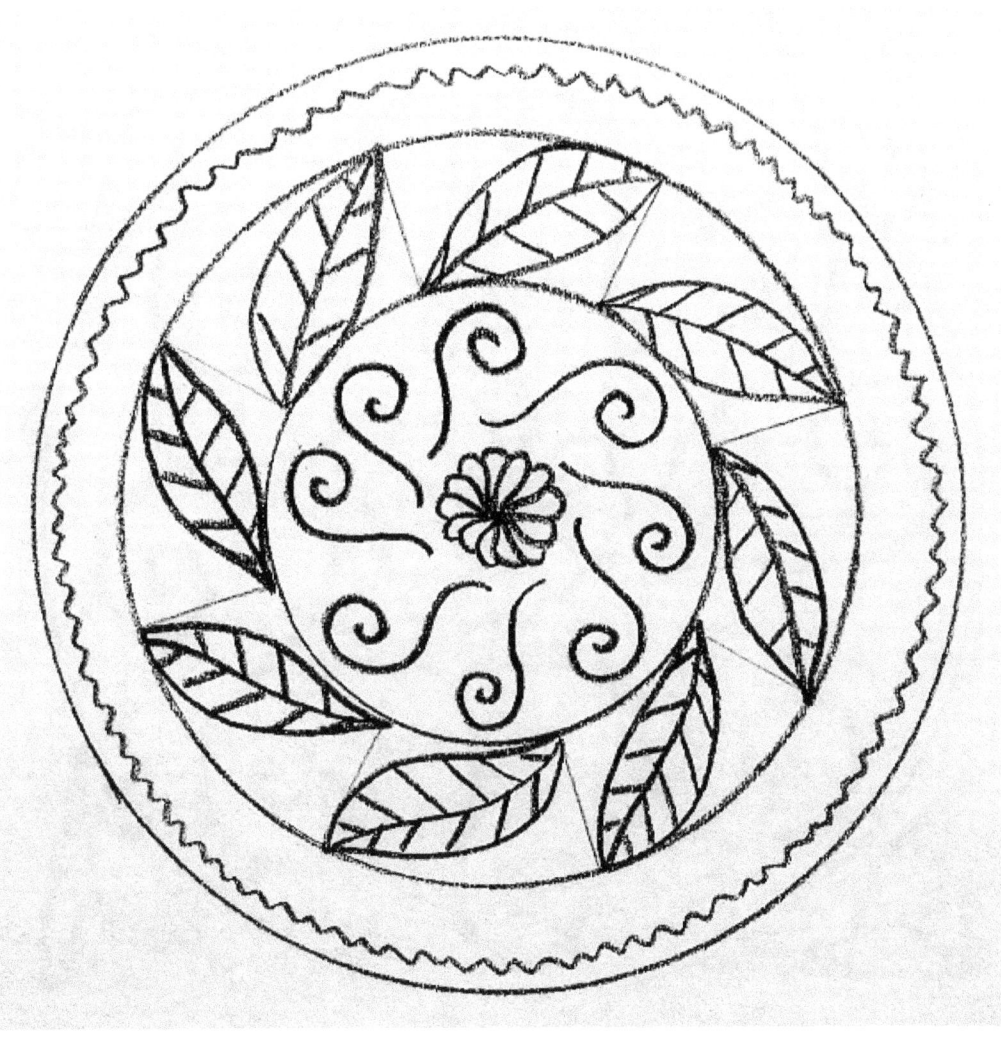

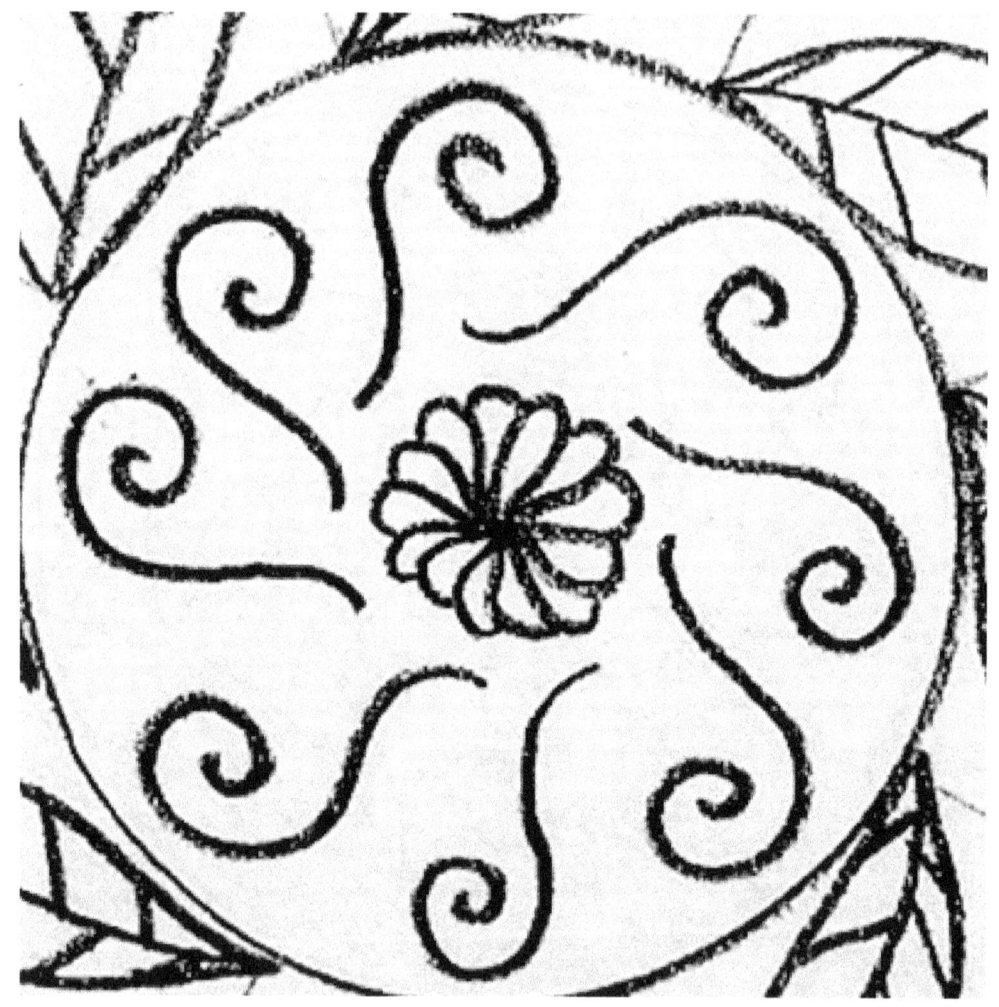

- Because this mandala is more flowing and angled, you might need to turn your paper as you work around the circle.

- There are twelve petals on your center flower. Try to make them as even in width and length as you can. Draw it around your center point.

- When creating your curled lines, start at the bottom of the line with a smooth sweep, making your top curl be centered in each pie piece. There should be eight curled lines to match your eight leaves.

- Don't worry if it isn't perfect, that is what gives your mandala charm. However, try to keep your curls at the top approximately the same size for balance in your mandala.

Step 6: Filling in the Details

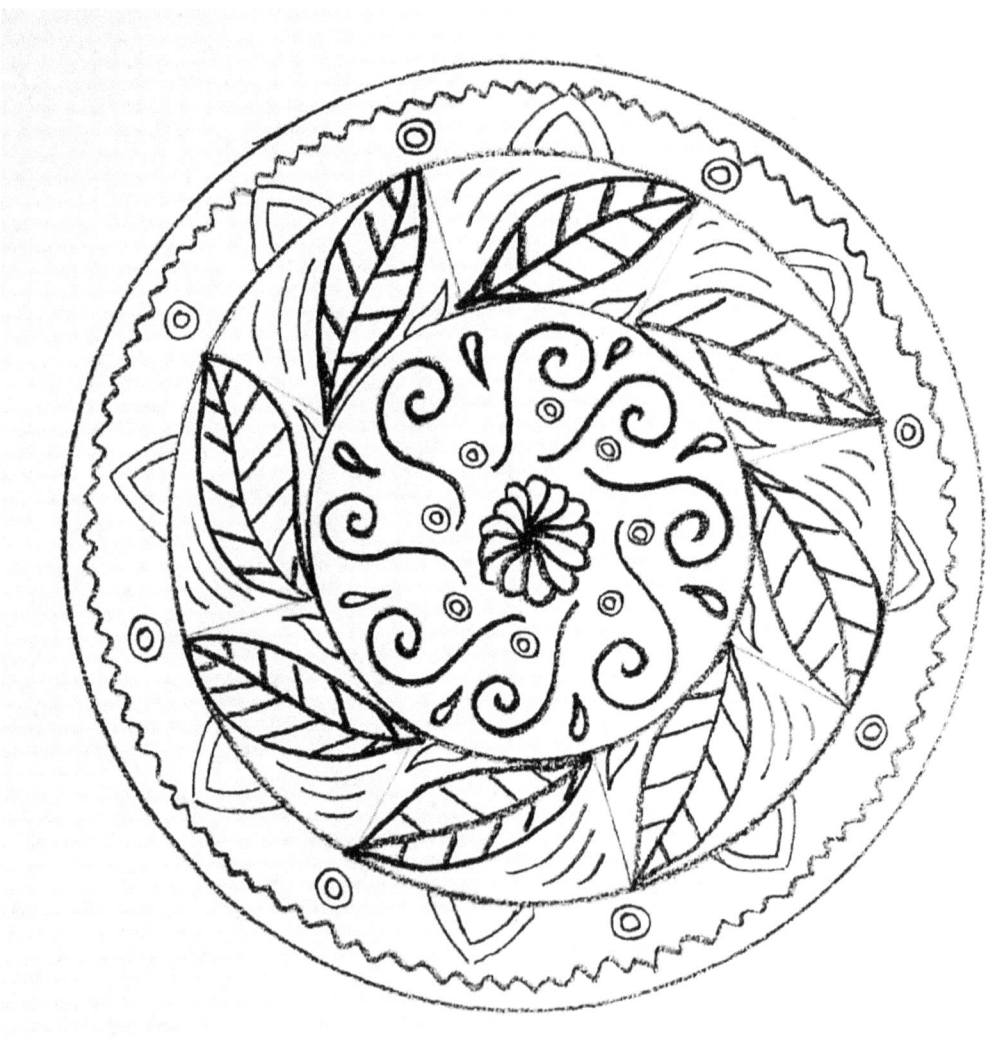

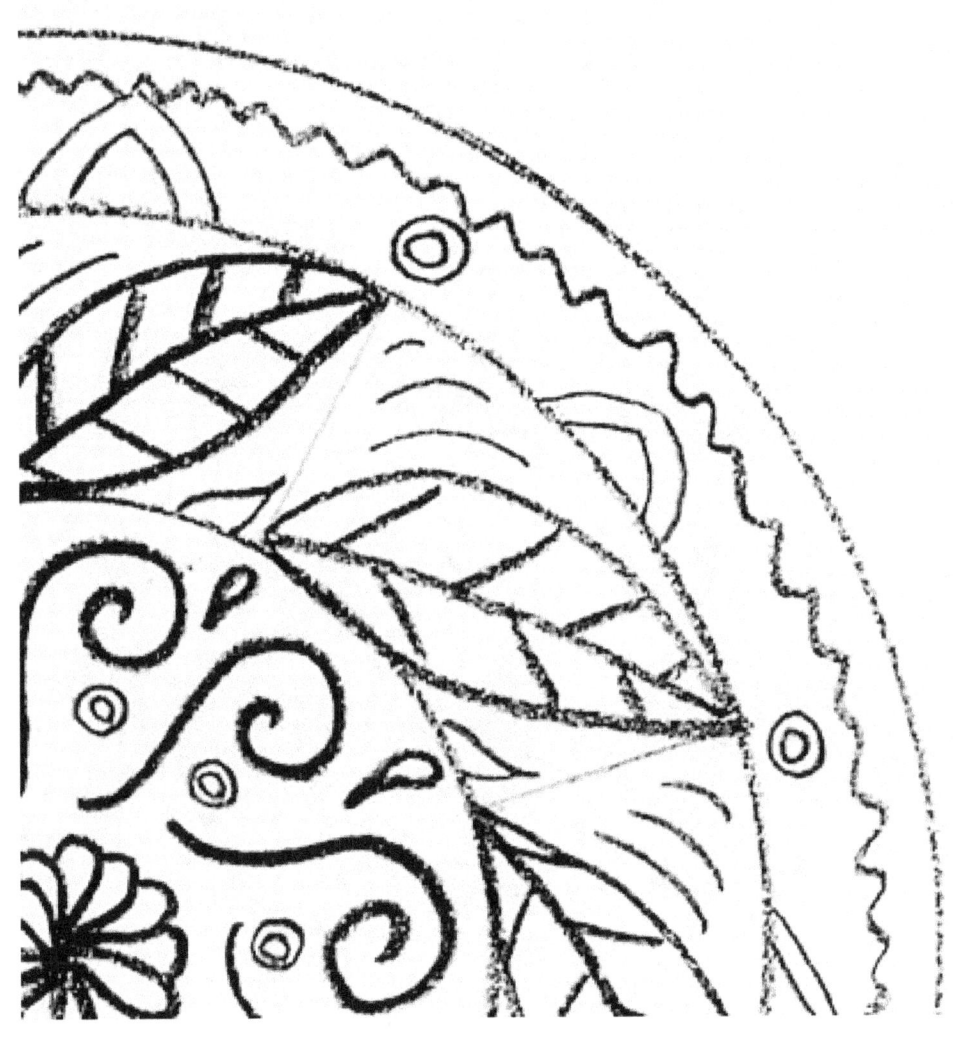

- Working from the center out, draw a double open dot between every curl. Try to place them in approximately the same place at the bottom of each curled line.

- Between the curls, draw a teardrop. There should be eight double open dots and eight teardrops.

- In the pie pieces, draw three lines to round the top of each leaf, making the top line the shortest and each one to follow just a little longer. At the bottom of the leaf in the bottom right corner of each pie piece, draw a small open leaf. This one will have no stems.

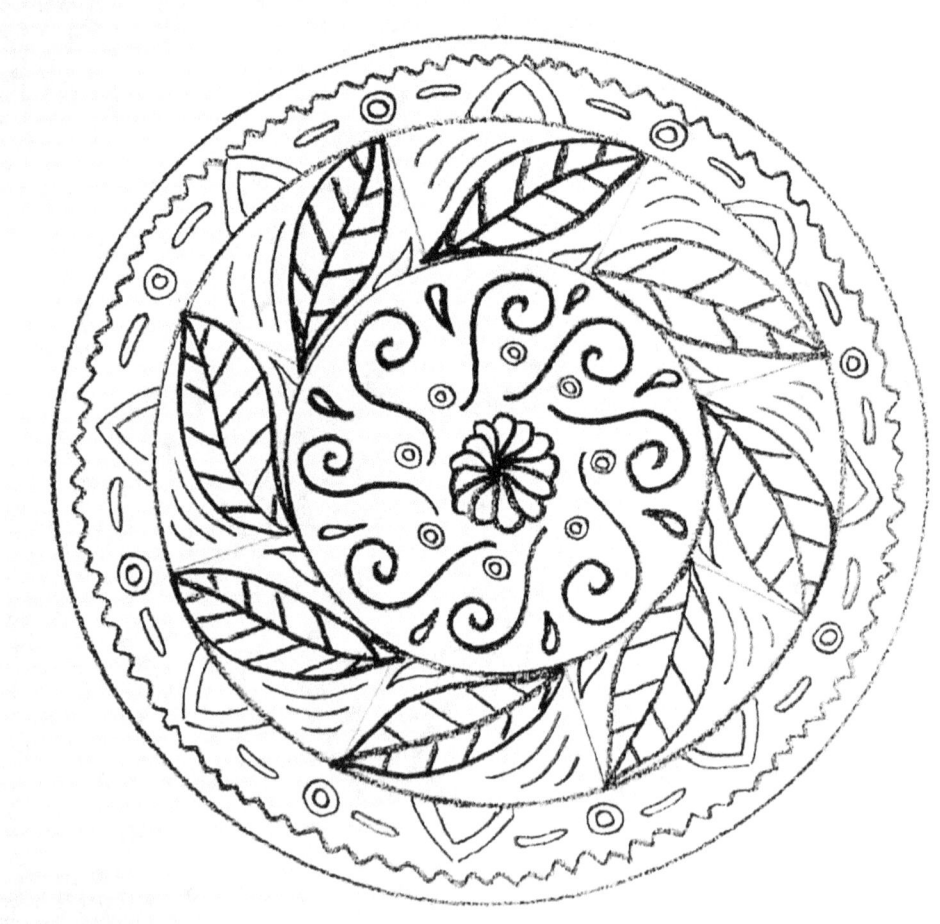

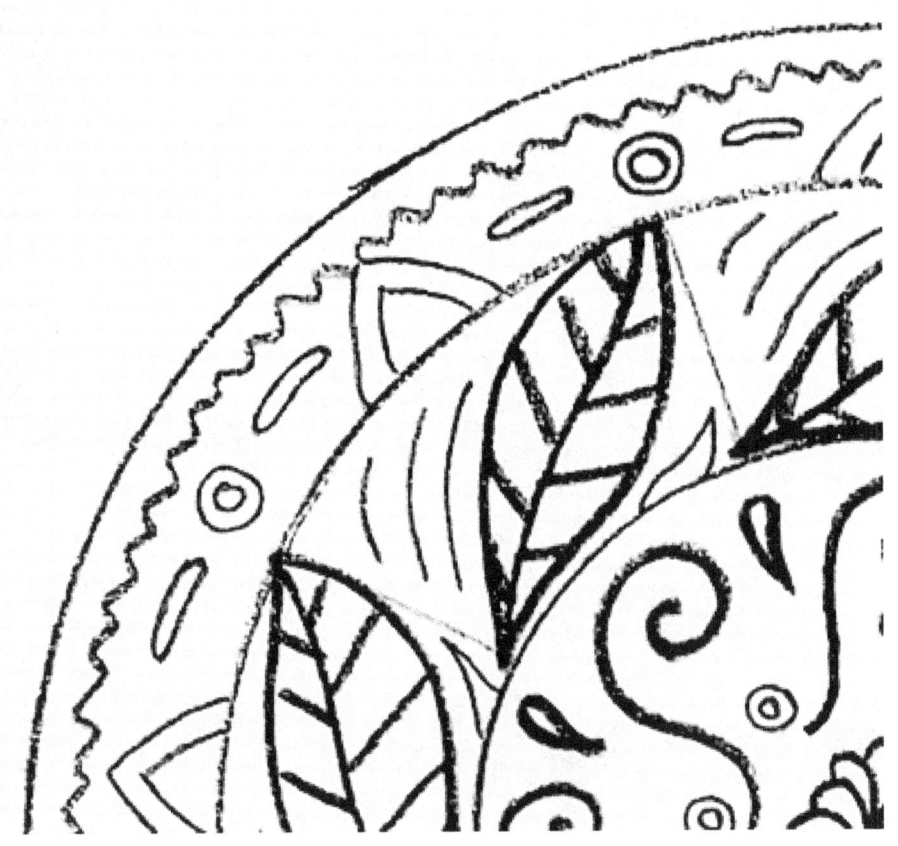

- At the center top of each pie piece, draw a double tent shape, but leave it open. You will notice that most of these shapes have not been colored in to give the mandala a beautiful open and flowing appearance.

- The top of the tent shapes should not quite touch the wiggly line, but go a little higher than half of the top circle.

- At the top of the pie piece lines, draw a double open dot. These dots should be approximately halfway between the wiggly line and the top circle line. Then add your double open dash lines on either side.

- Notice that all these lines are not filled in, and they do not touch other lines. This keeps the mandala open and creates more white space between the designs.

Chapter 3: A Kaleidoscope Design

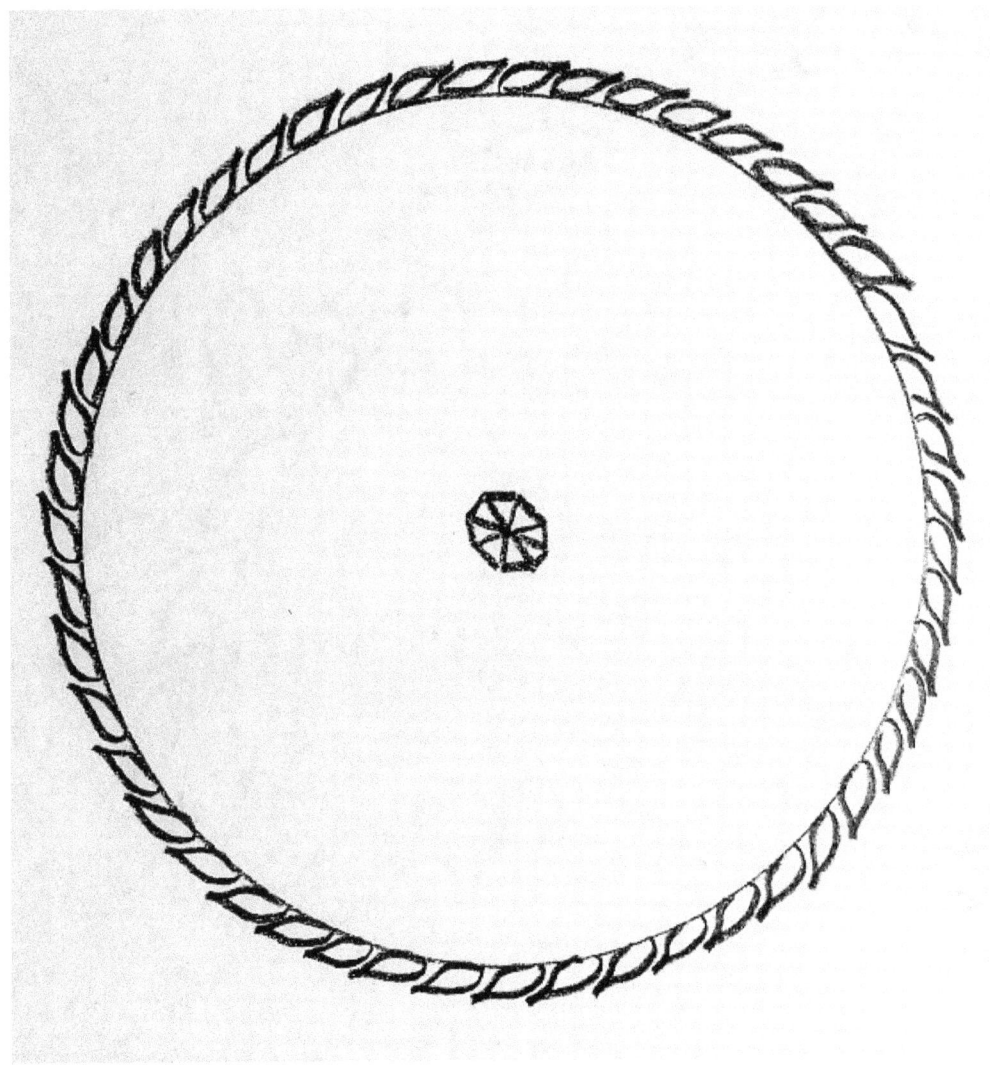

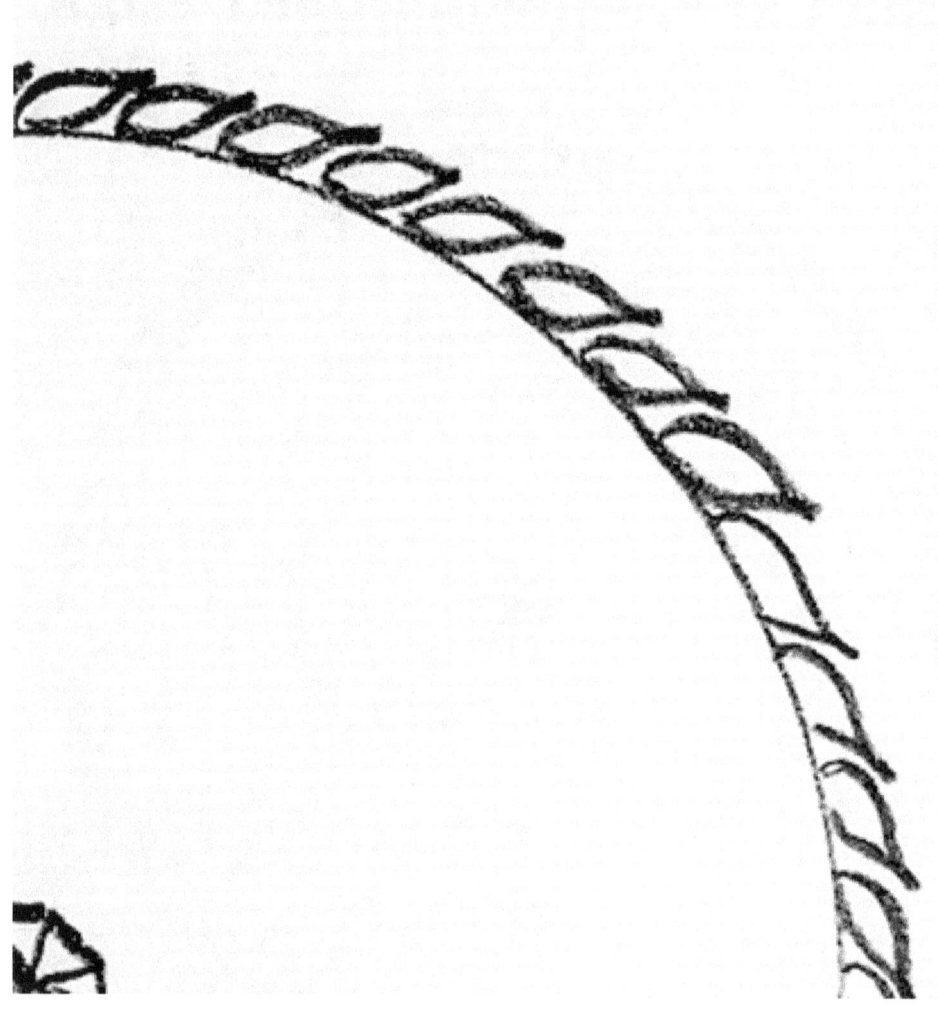

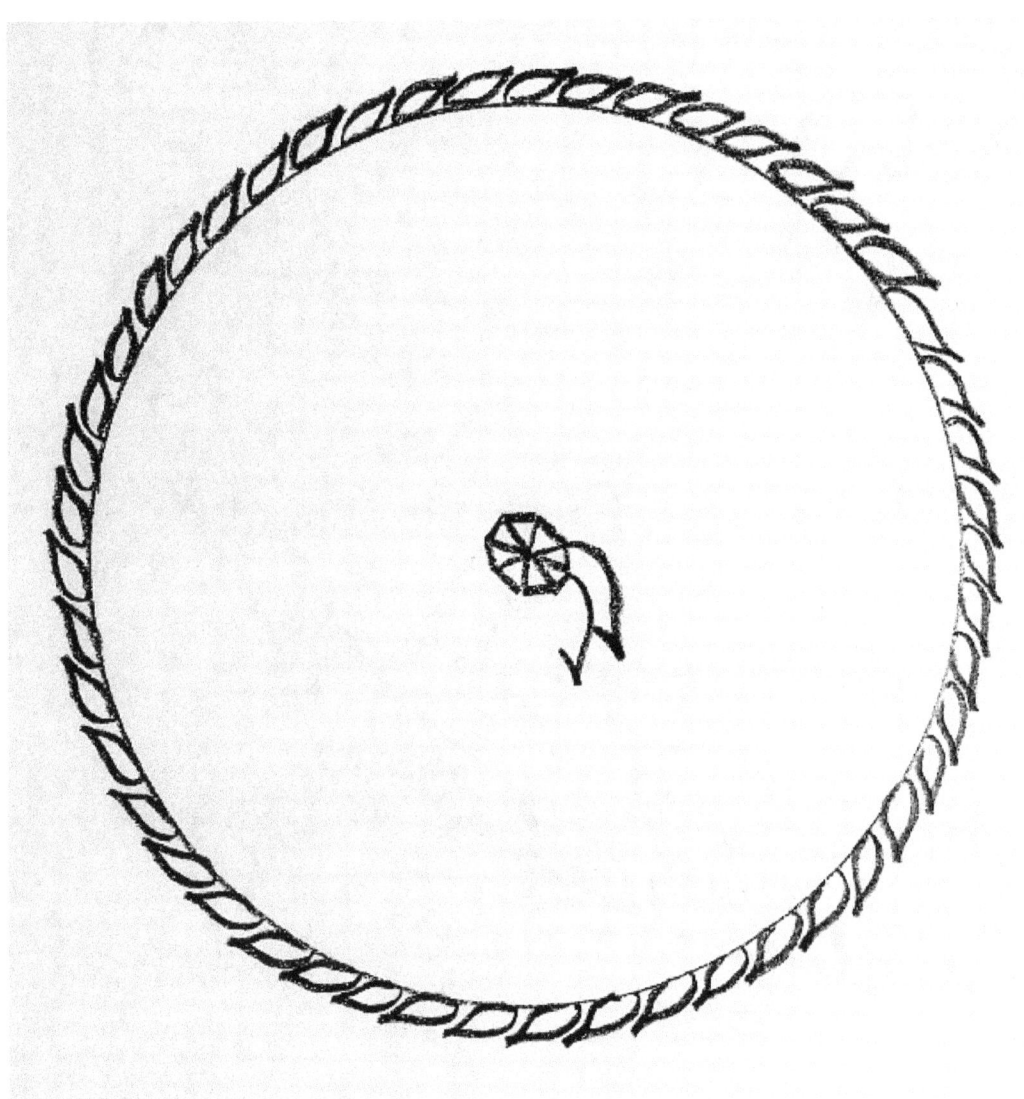

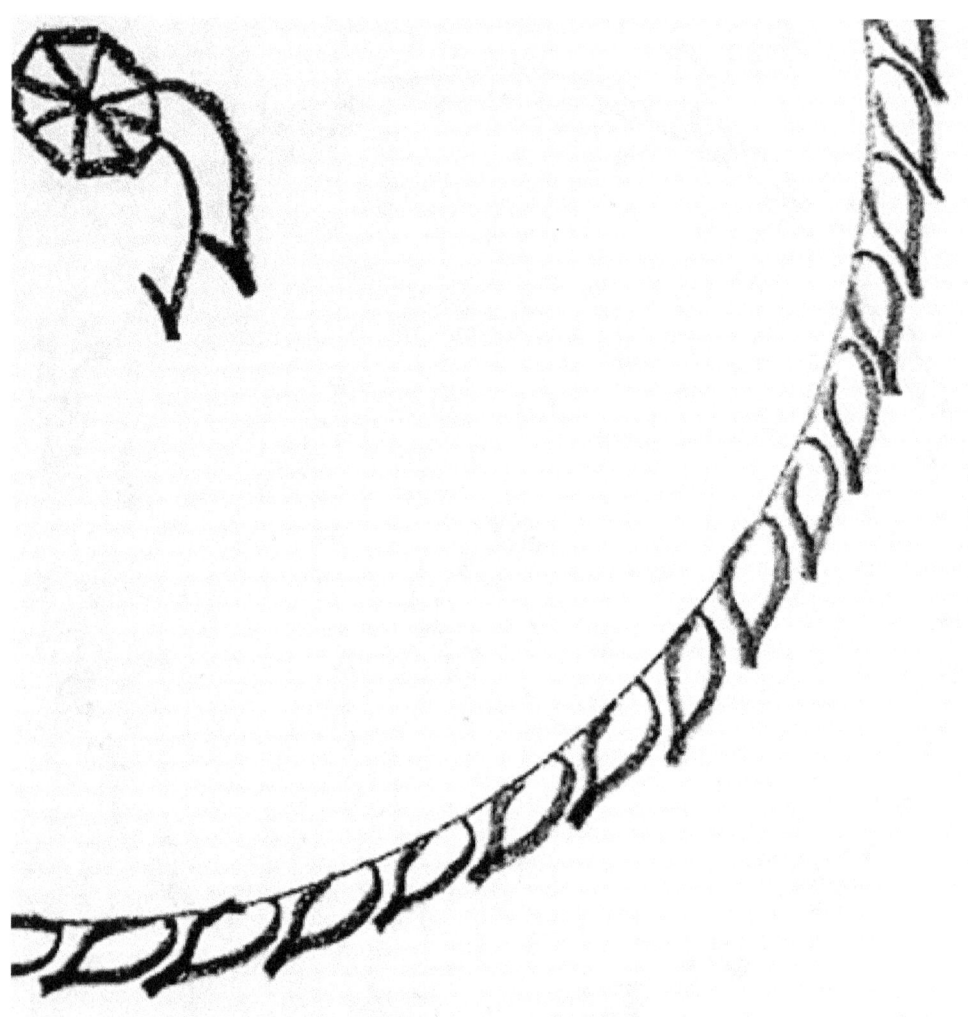

Step 1: More Free-Hand Style

- Begin with your outside circle.

- Draw a teardrop shape with the wider end touching the outside circle. You won't need to count these shapes, just line the outside circle with them.

- Find your center point and, using your transparent ruler, draw an eight-pointed star through the center point.

- Connect the star points with a straight line at the end. Your center point will be in the shape of an octagon—or eight-sided.

- From each of the octagon star lines, draw an open line curving reverse "C" line with a barb on the end. Make sure the barbed line goes about one-third through the circle. Then repeat the process with each octagon star line. The back of the reverse "Cs' should touch the barb of the one before it. Continue all the way around the octagon shape.

Step 2: Adding the Details

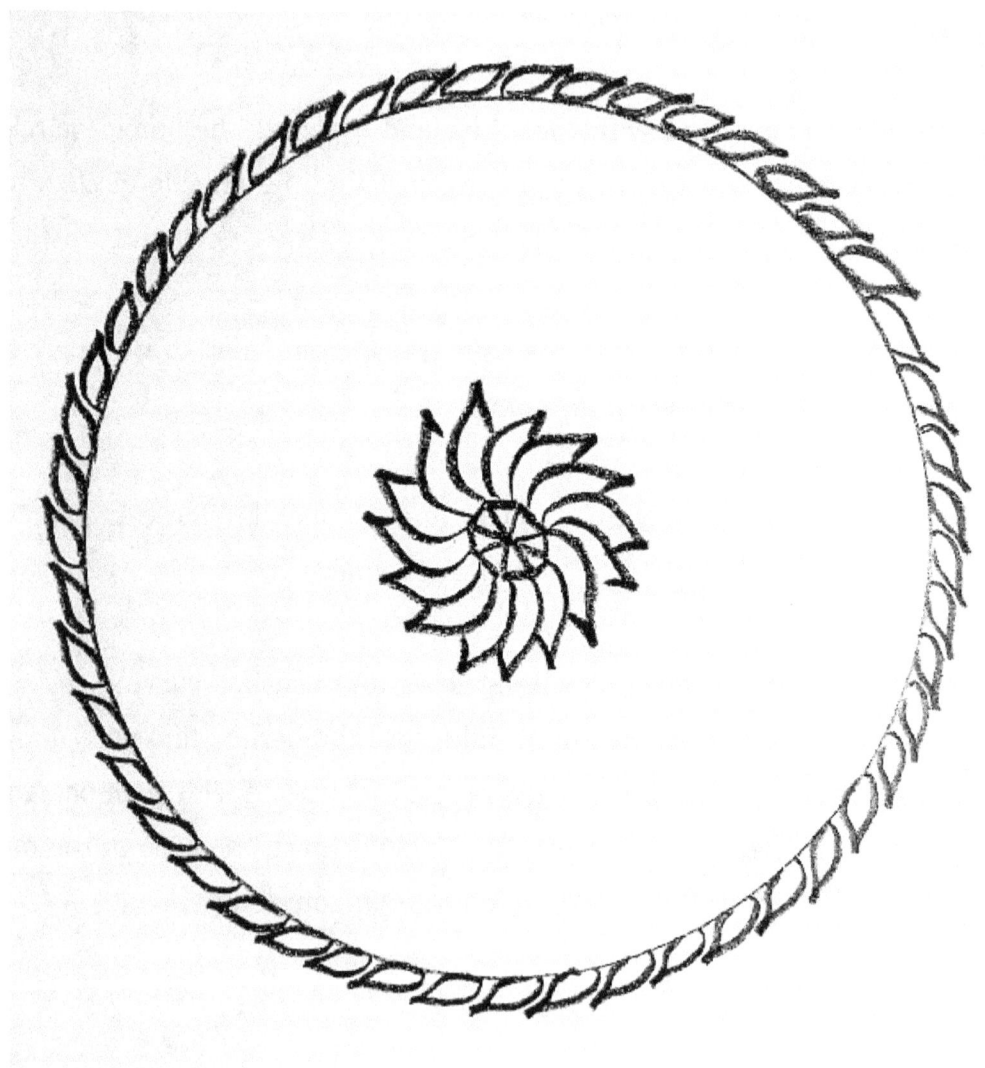

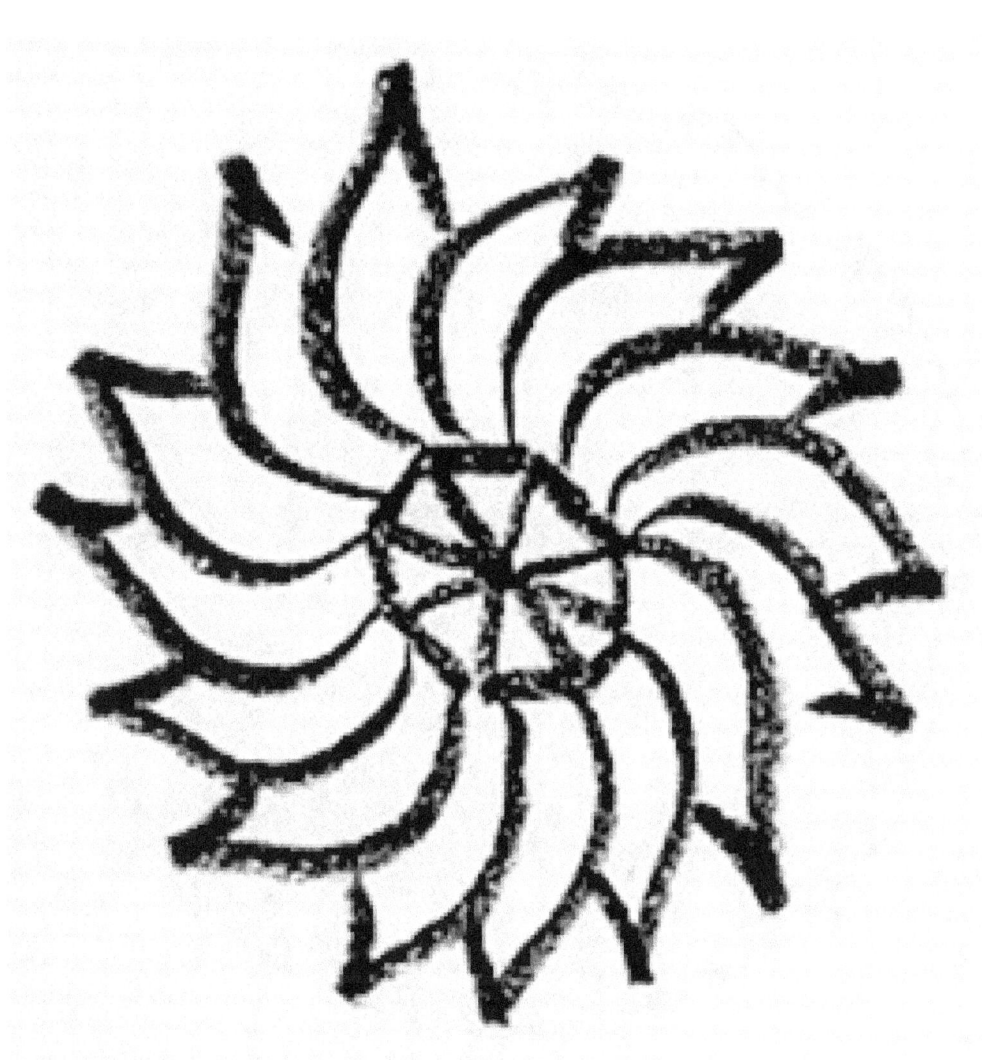

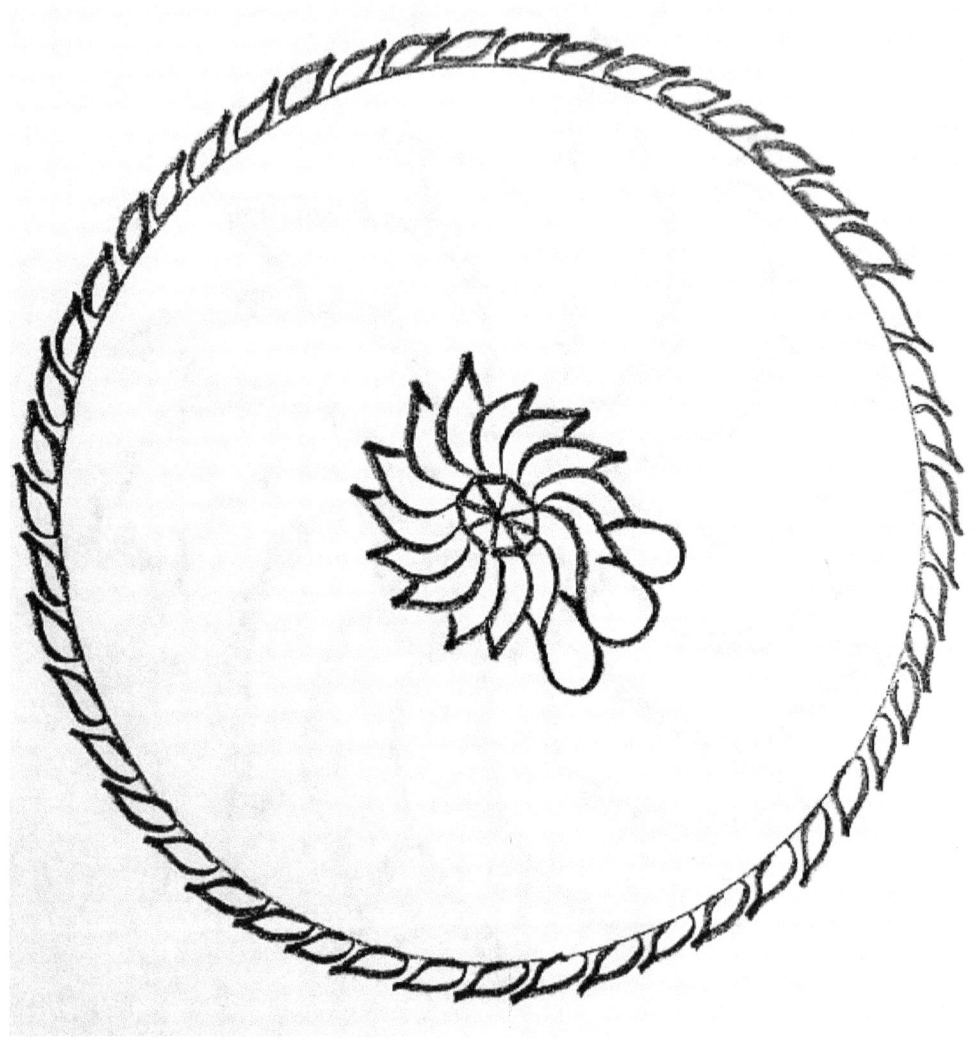

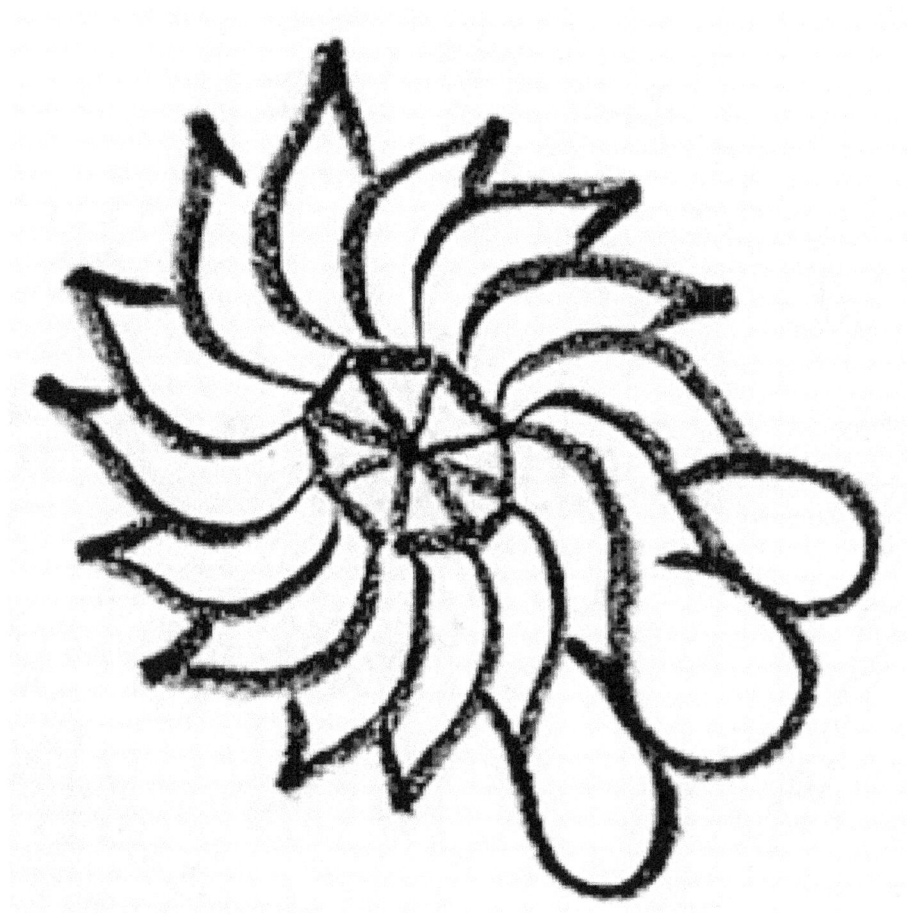

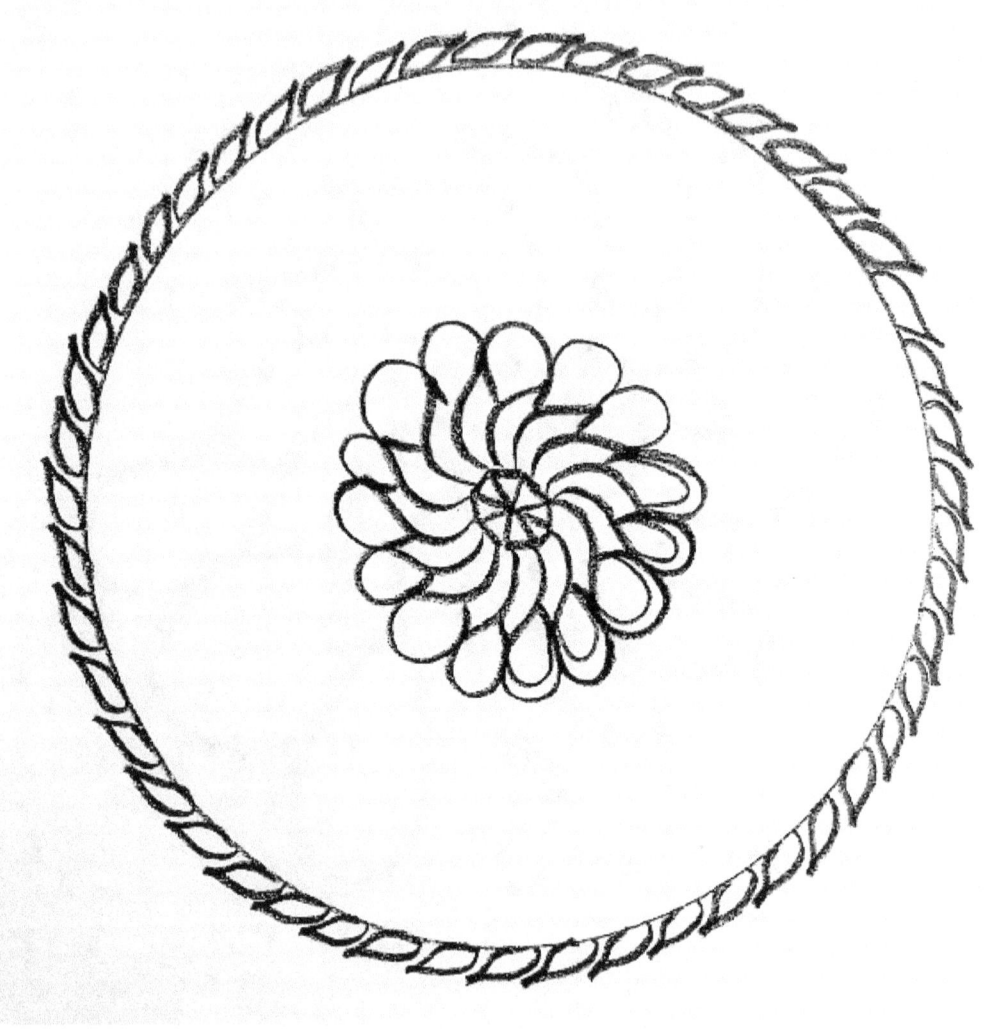

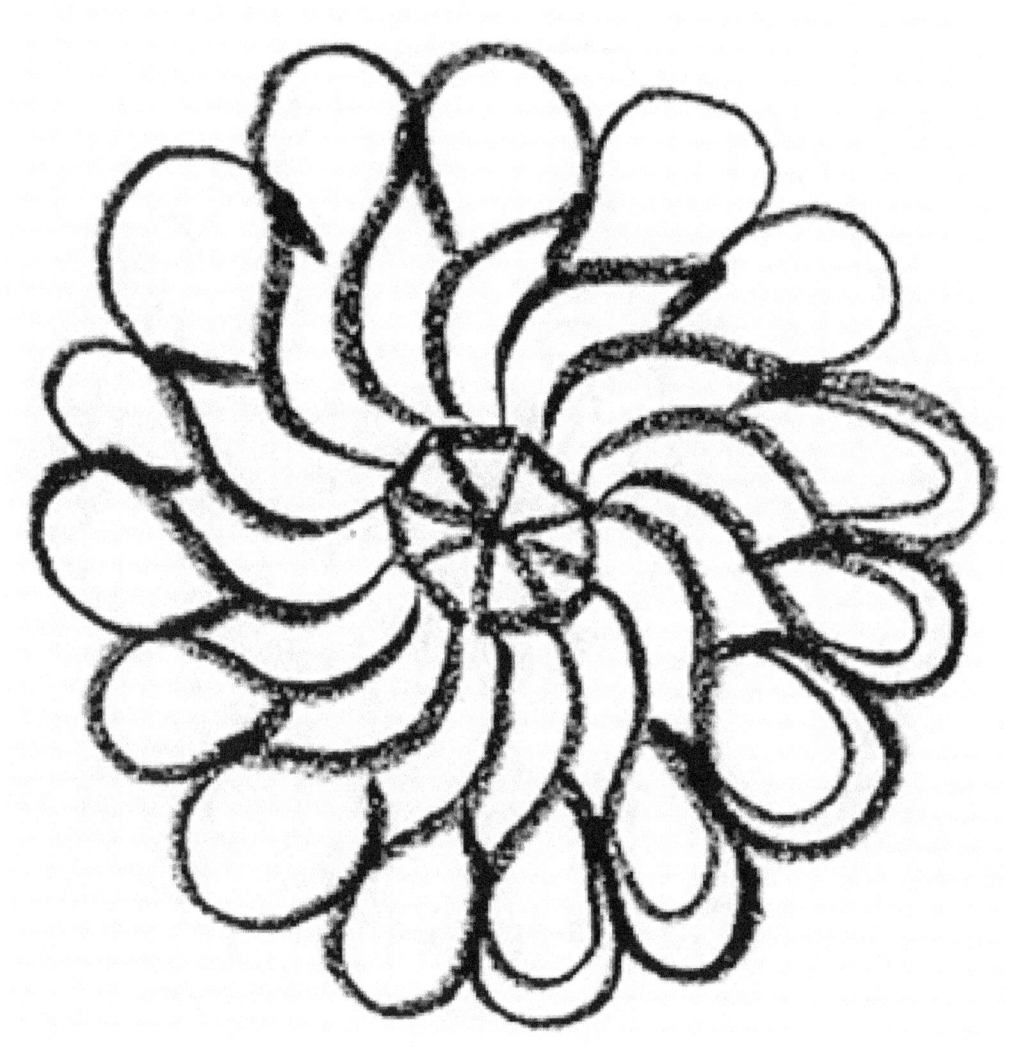

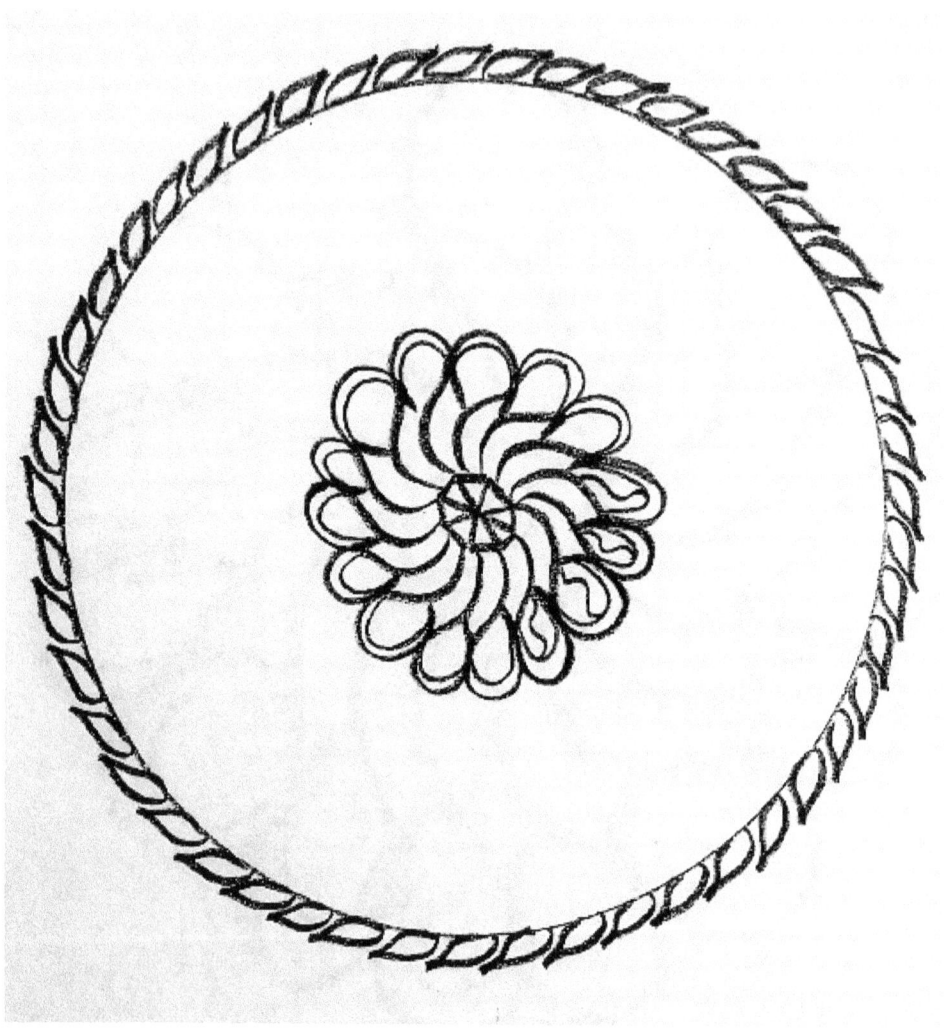

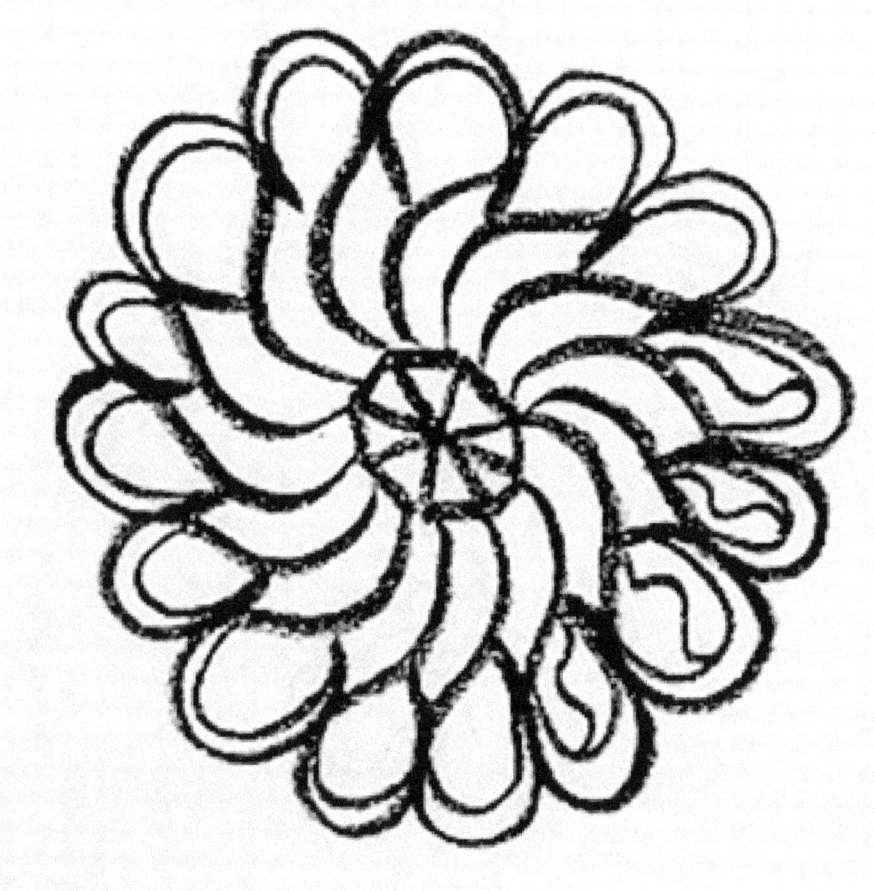

- Add bulbs at the end of each leaf, then follow that with another line to go around the outside of each bulb.

- Now divide the inside bulb into two pieces with a wiggly line down the center of each bulb.

Step 3: Building on to the Pattern

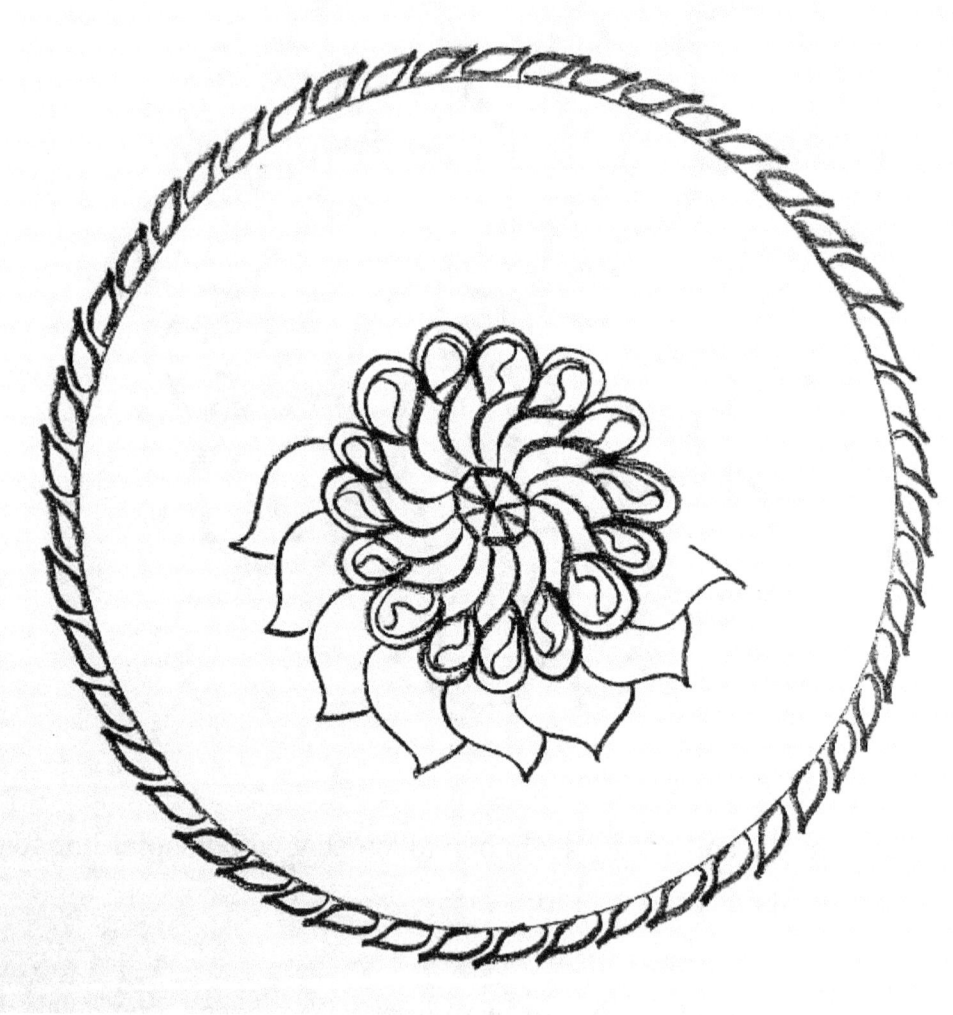

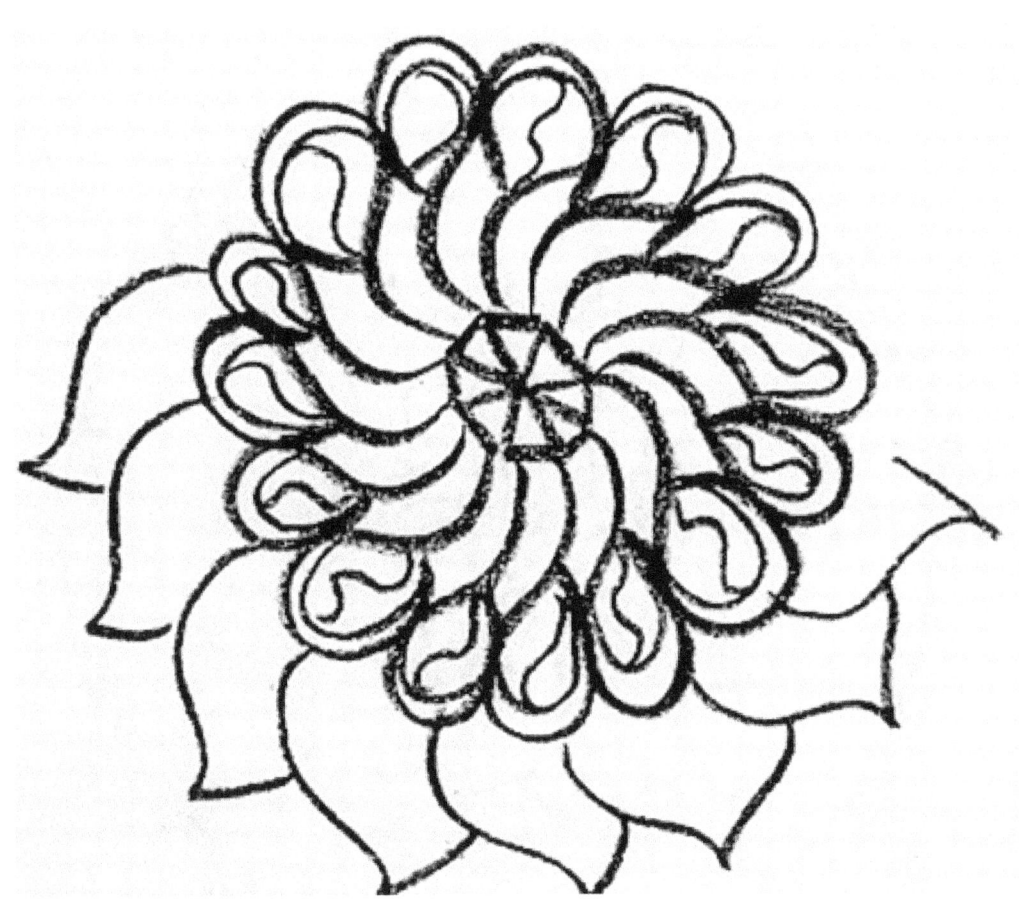

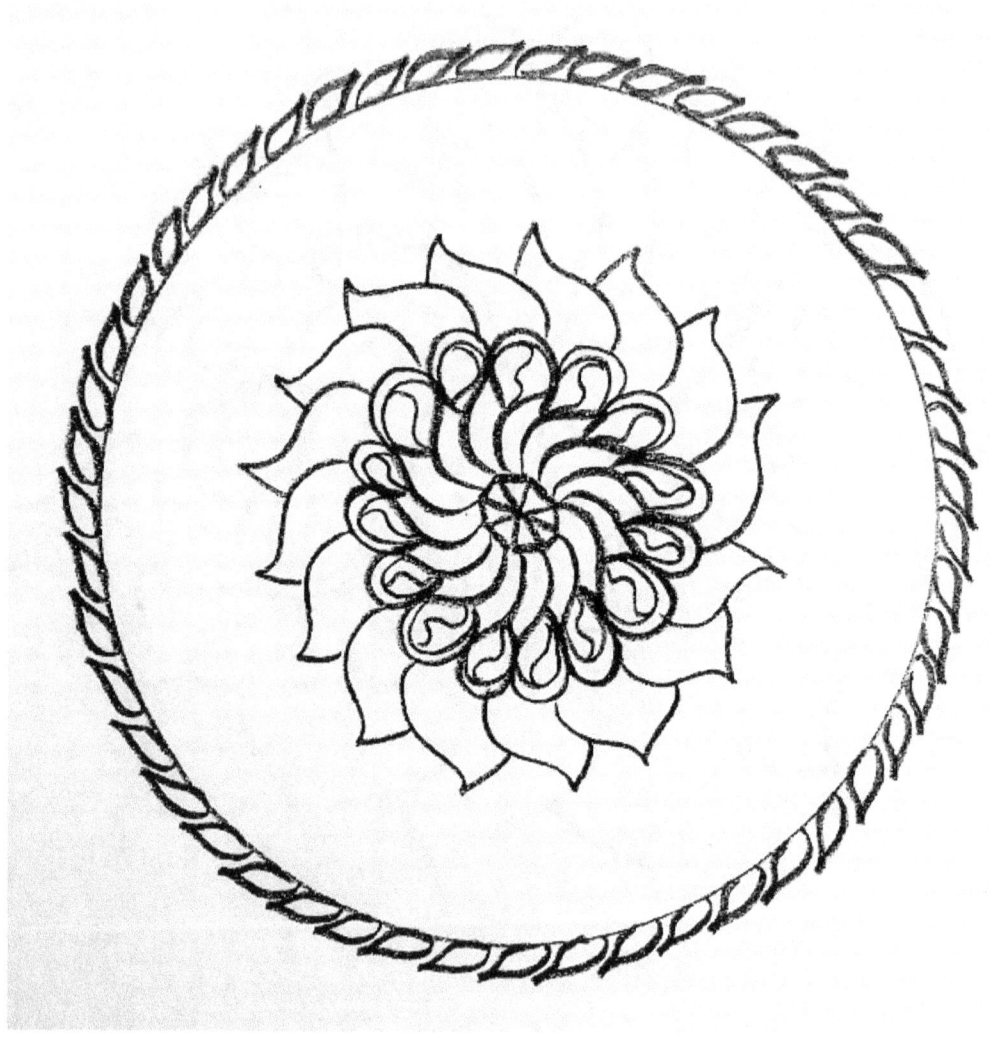

- Just as you did the smaller reverse "Cs," now you want to draw a line pattern like a regular forward "C" with a barb at the end. The "Cs" will be fuller and move in the opposite direction than the previous ones.

- Each larger leaf should begin in the center of the bulb, with the point of the barb at the center of the next bulb.

- Follow this pattern around all the bulbs. To keep the leaves going in the right direction, you may need to twirl your paper. Try to keep the same size of the leaves all the way around.

Step 4: Creating the Outer Leaf Details

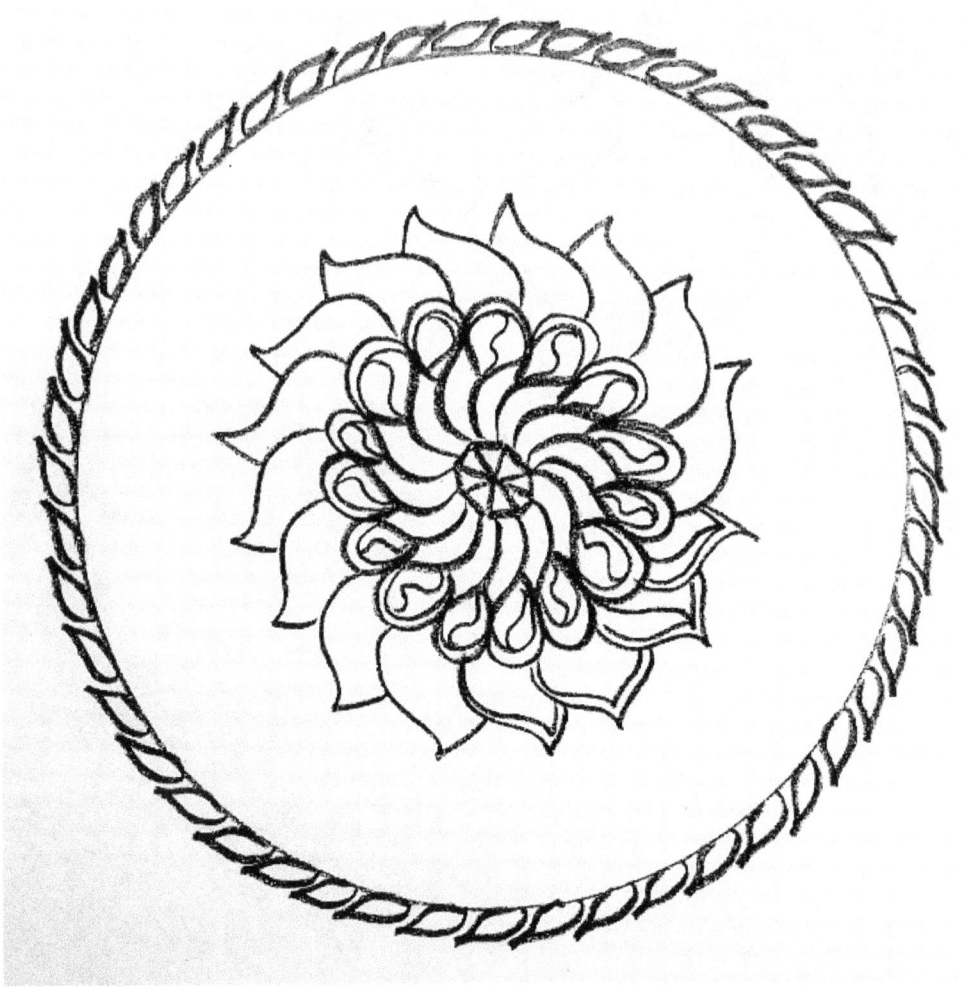

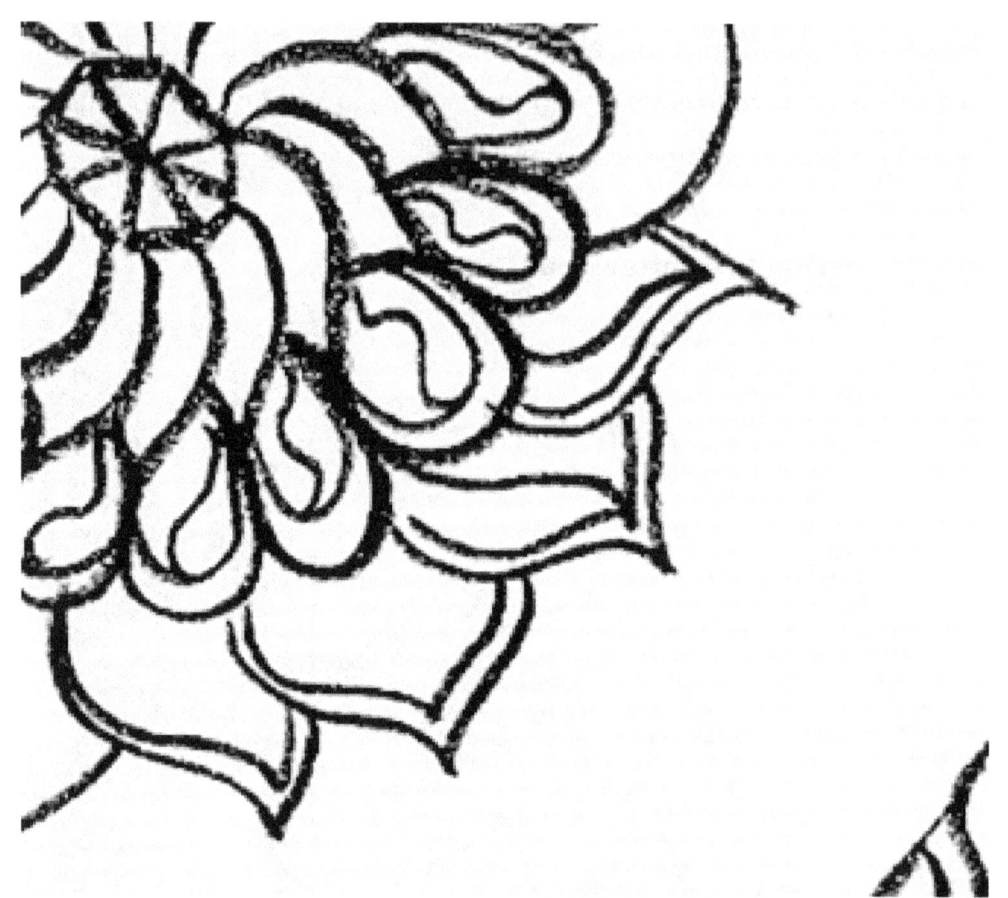

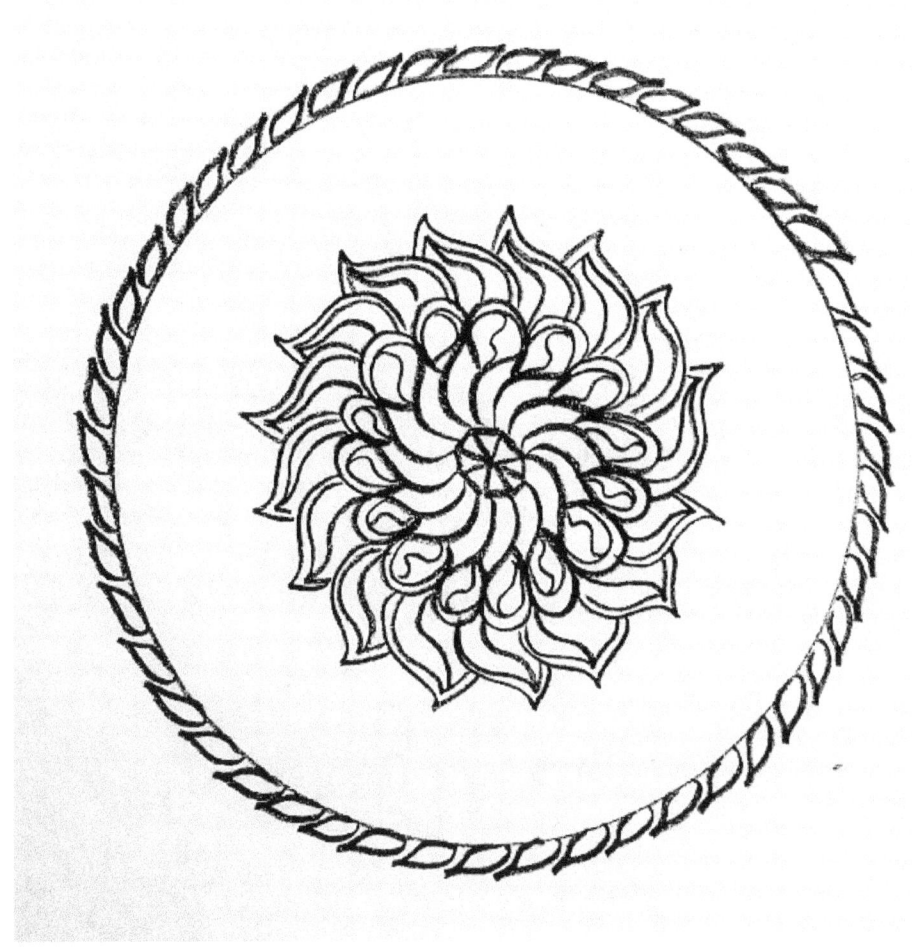

- To give the larger leaves more detail and curve, outline the "C" and the barb, and then draw a line from the point of the leaf down to the bottom middle of the leaf.

- Your mandala should almost look as though it has movement now with the leaves angled in the opposite direction. It should give your center point the appearance of lifting off the page.

- The additional lines begin to give your mandala depth and movement.

- Continue adding in all the lines around the circle. Remember to turn your paper if it makes it easier to keep a proper angle to your lines.

Step 5: Continuing to Build the Circle

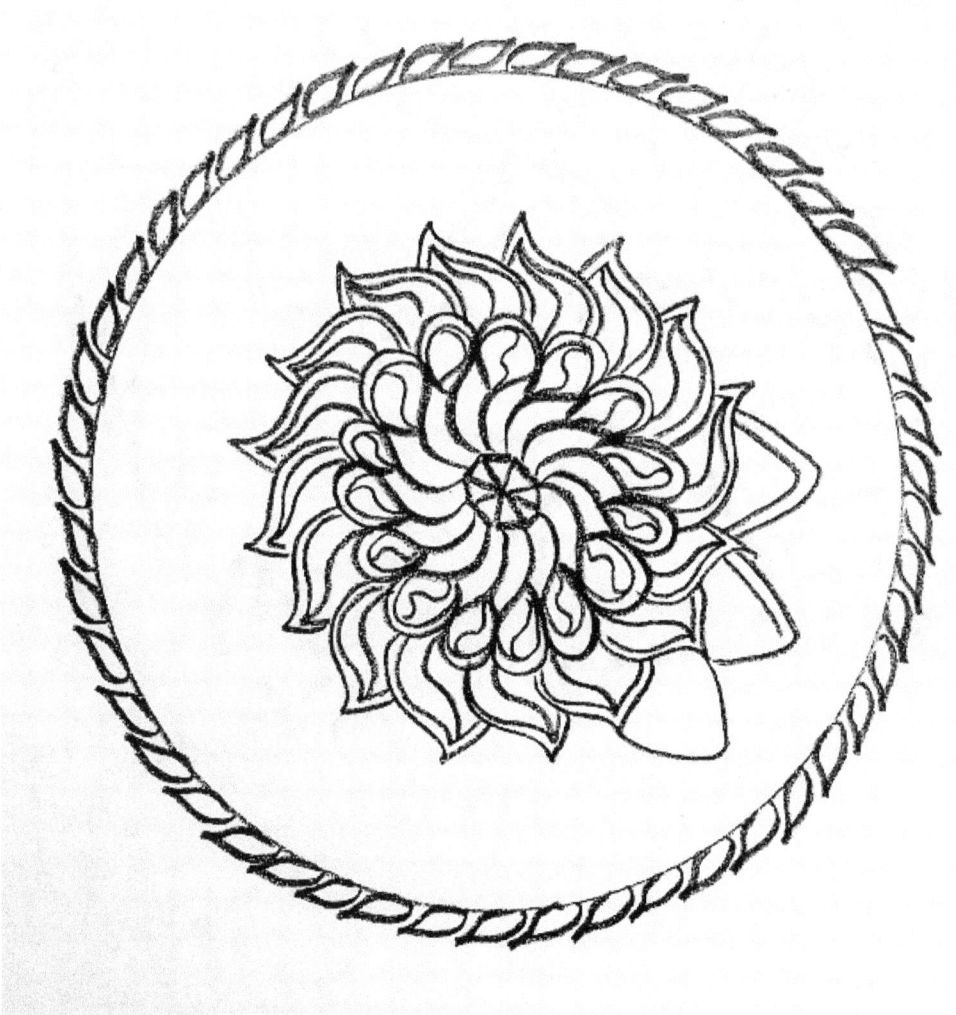

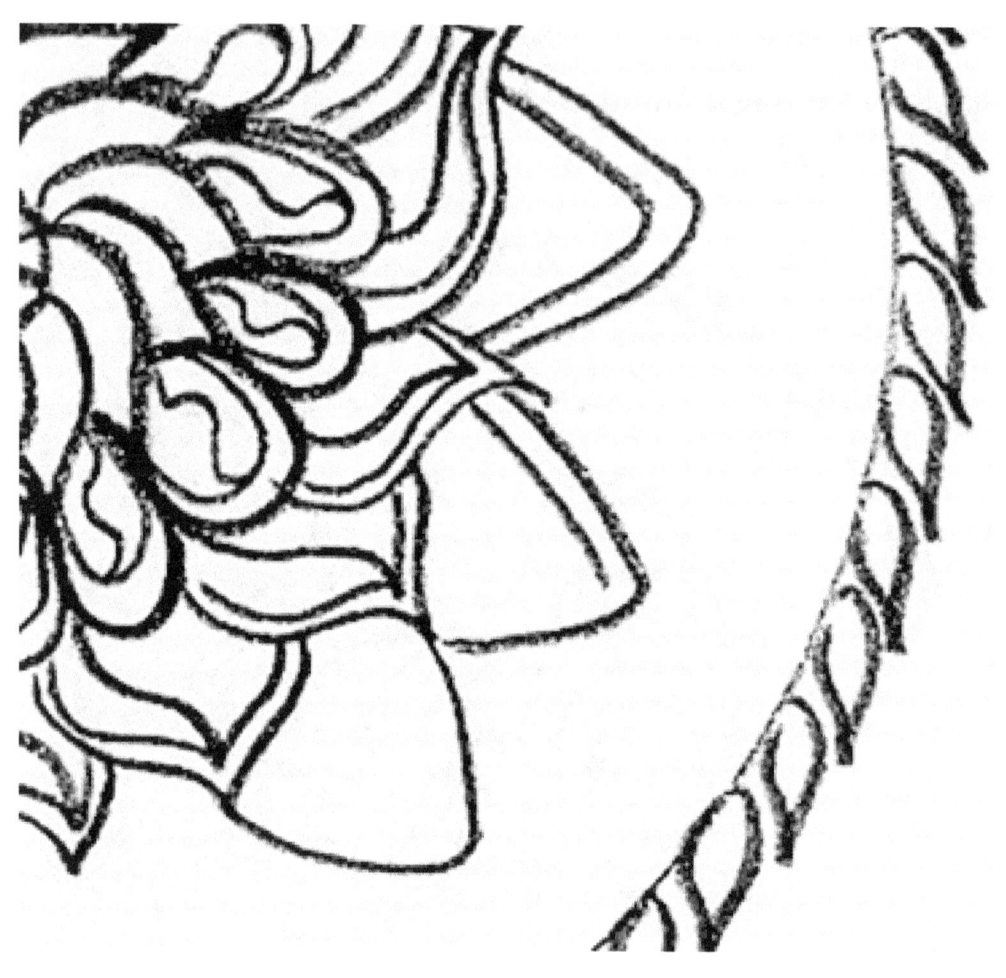

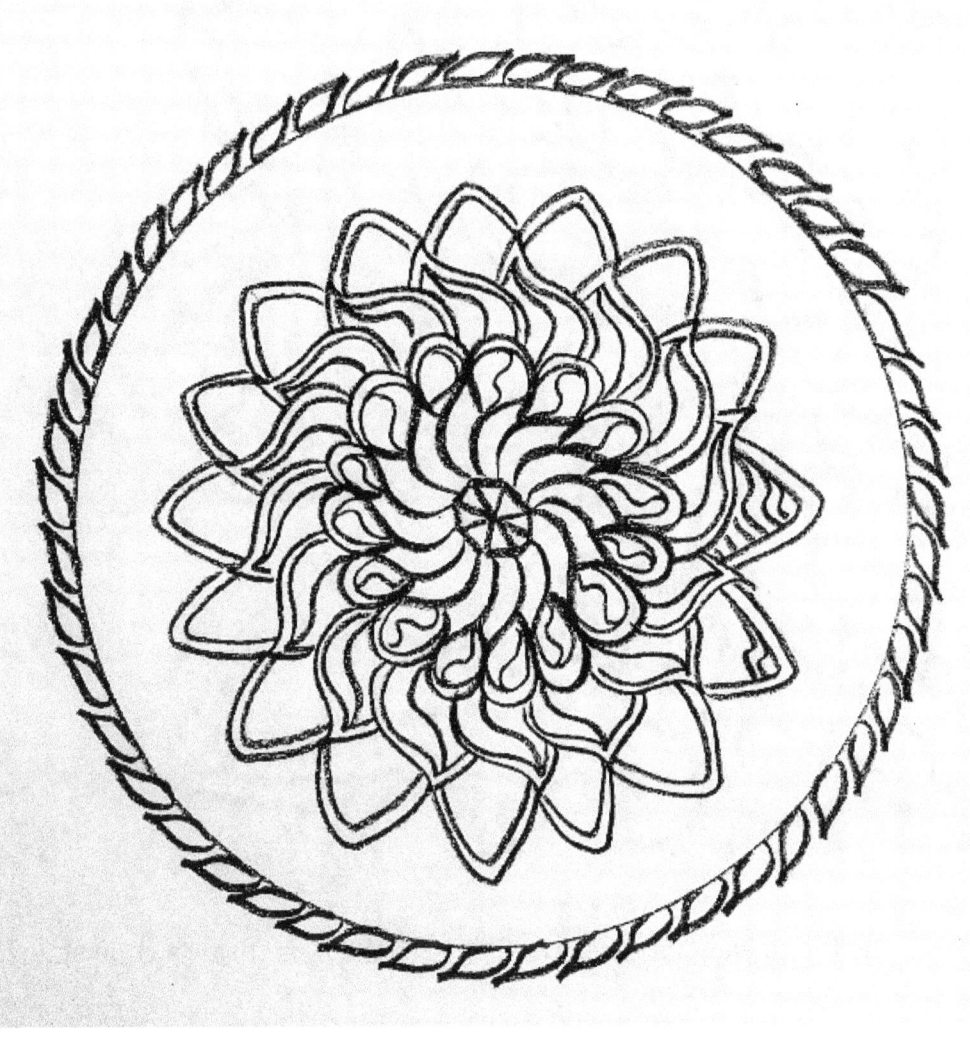

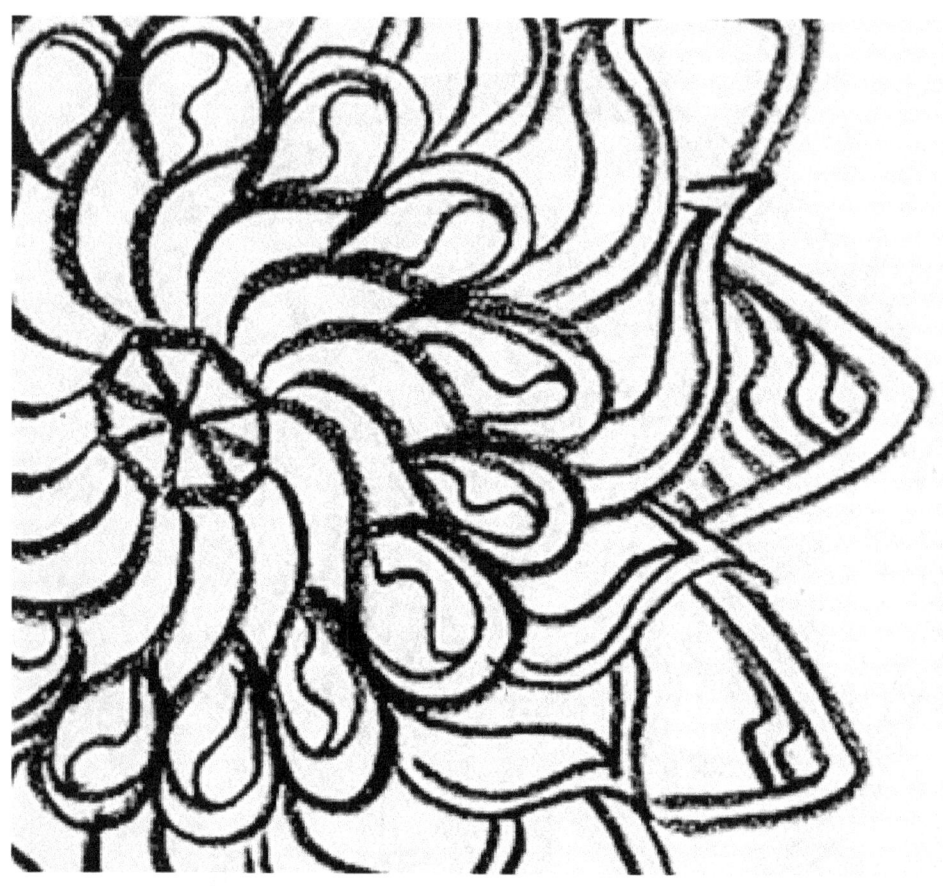

- From the top of each large leaf to the tip of the next, draw a cone shape.

- The cone shapes should take up about half of the space between the large leaves and the outside circle.

- Line each cone on the inside to create a border.

- Draw wavy lines inside each cone.

- You don't have to worry about how many wavy lines you draw, just try to keep them approximately the same distance apart. This will continue to give your mandala movement, balance, and interest.

- Repeat these patterns until you have gone all the way around the circle.

Step 6: Finishing the Outer Circle

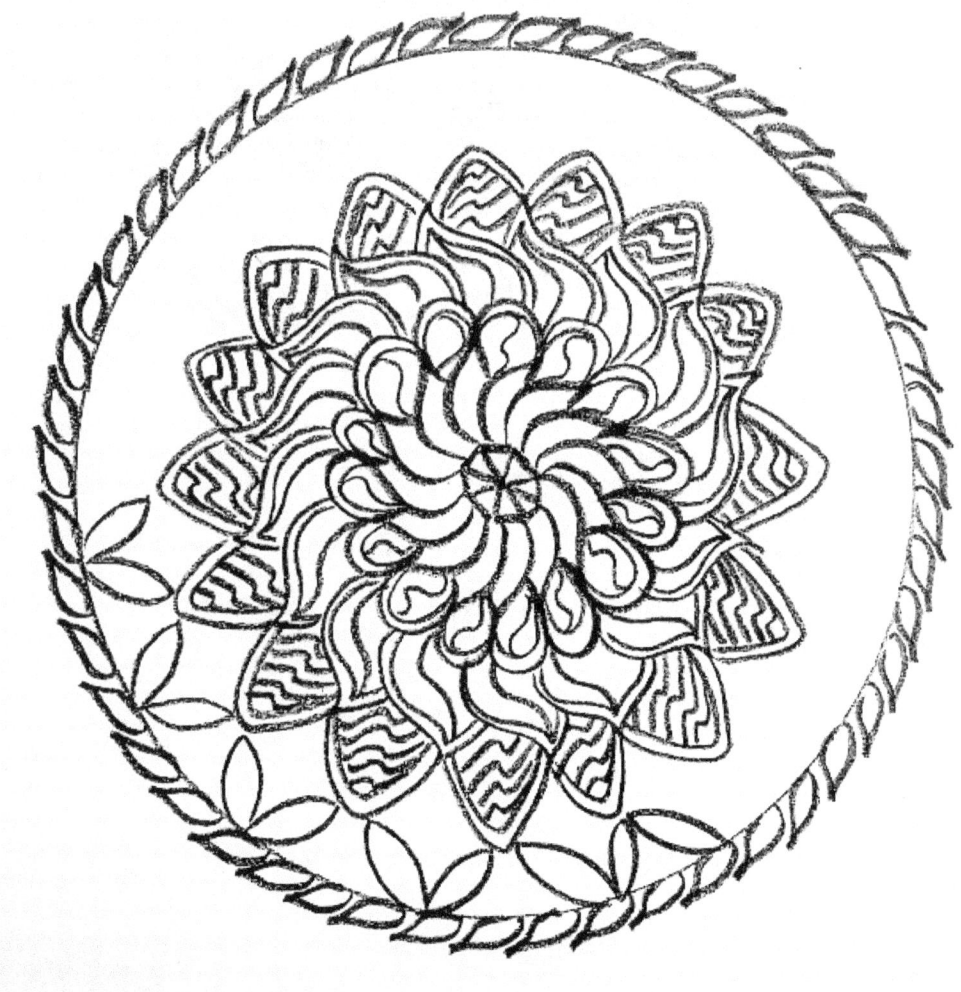

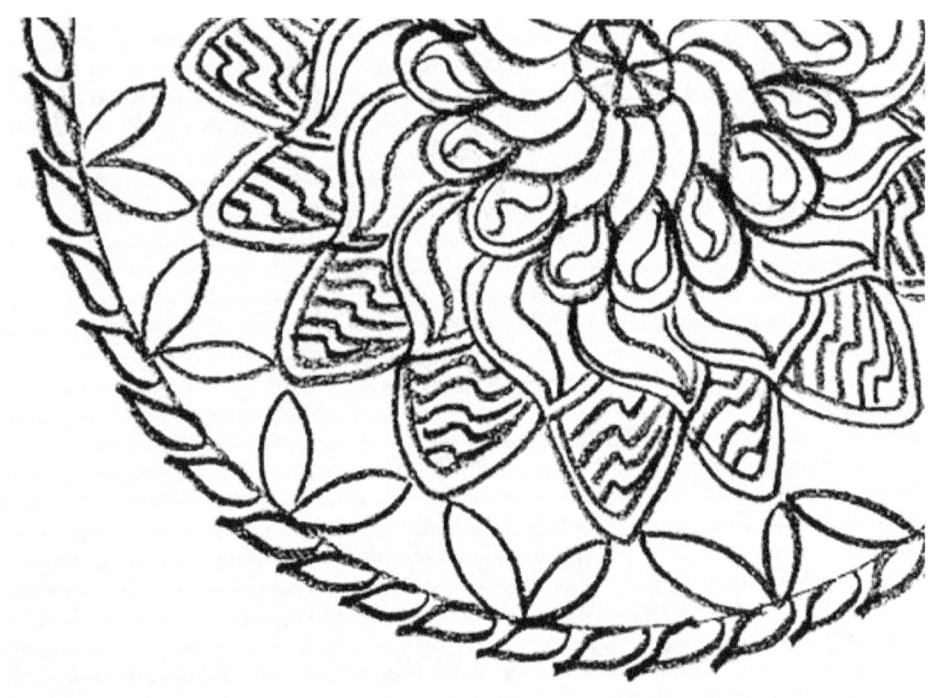

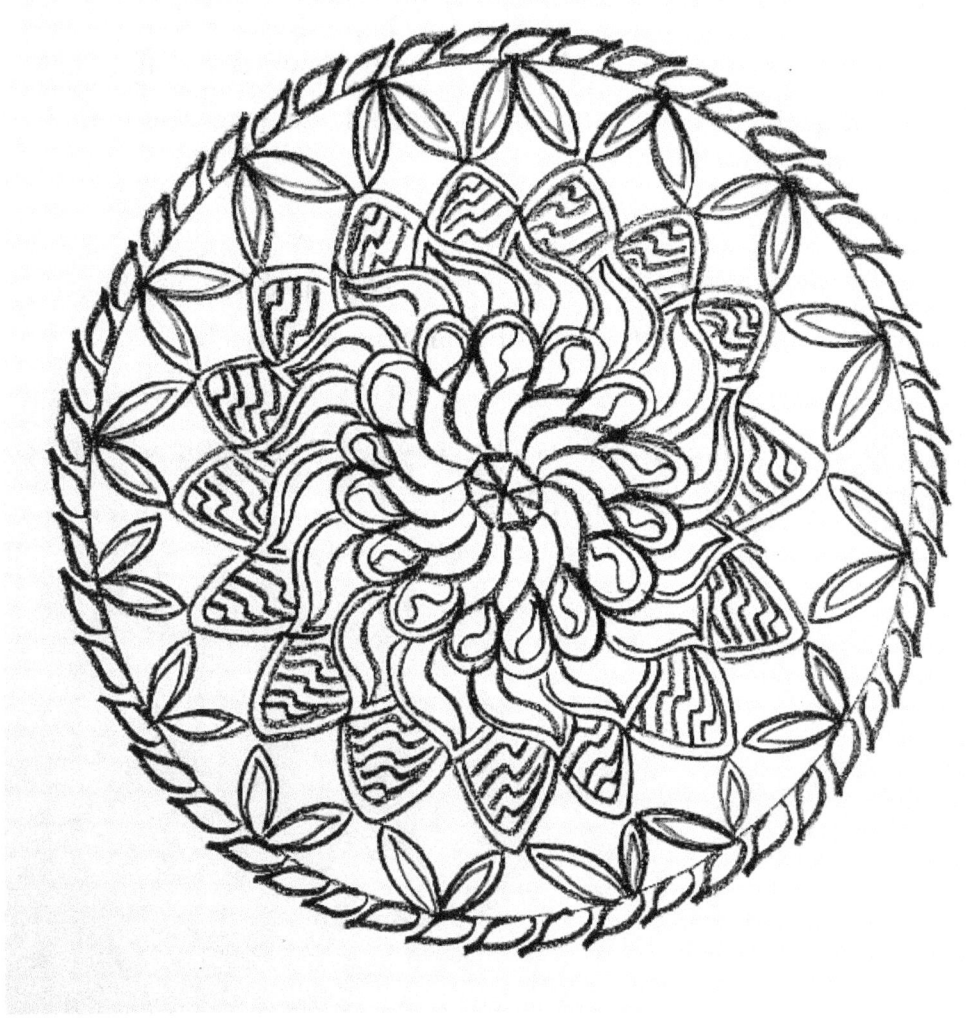

- Once you have completed drawing the cone shapes around the entire circle, then begin the outer leaves.

- Touching the outside circle, between each cone draw two leaves. They should touch at the base and flare out to almost touch each tip of the cone shapes.

- Once you have drawn the leaf shapes around the entire outer circle, Line the inside of the leaves for the last detail.

- Notice how the mandala looks raised—almost dimensional. That was created by taking the leaves and barbs just outside the center point in the opposite direction.

- The wavy lines on the outside leaves gives the mandala a flattened look in that area, almost as it were resting on those leaves.

- The fun thing about mandalas is that you can be creative with your details and create dimension and depth.

Chapter 4: Open Spaced Free-hand Mandala

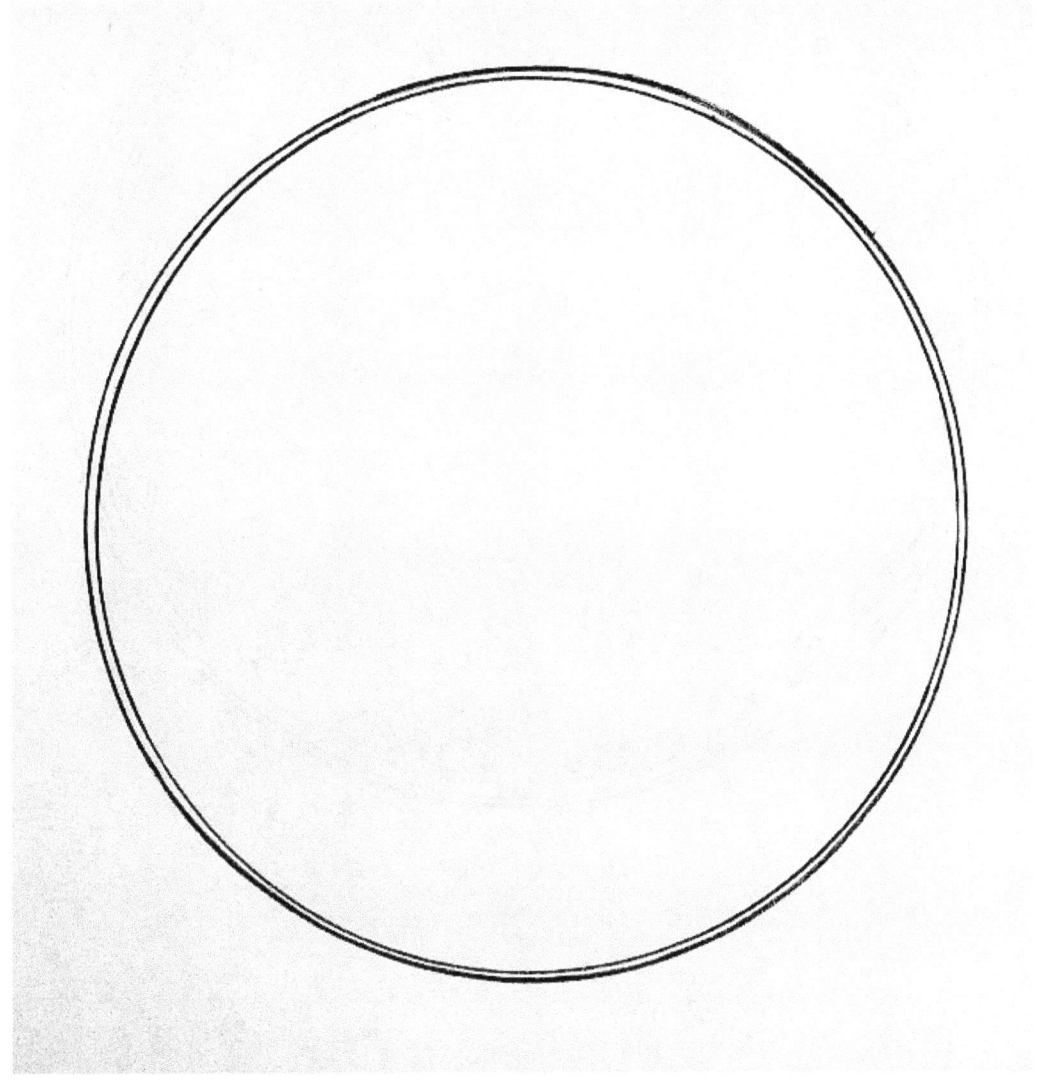

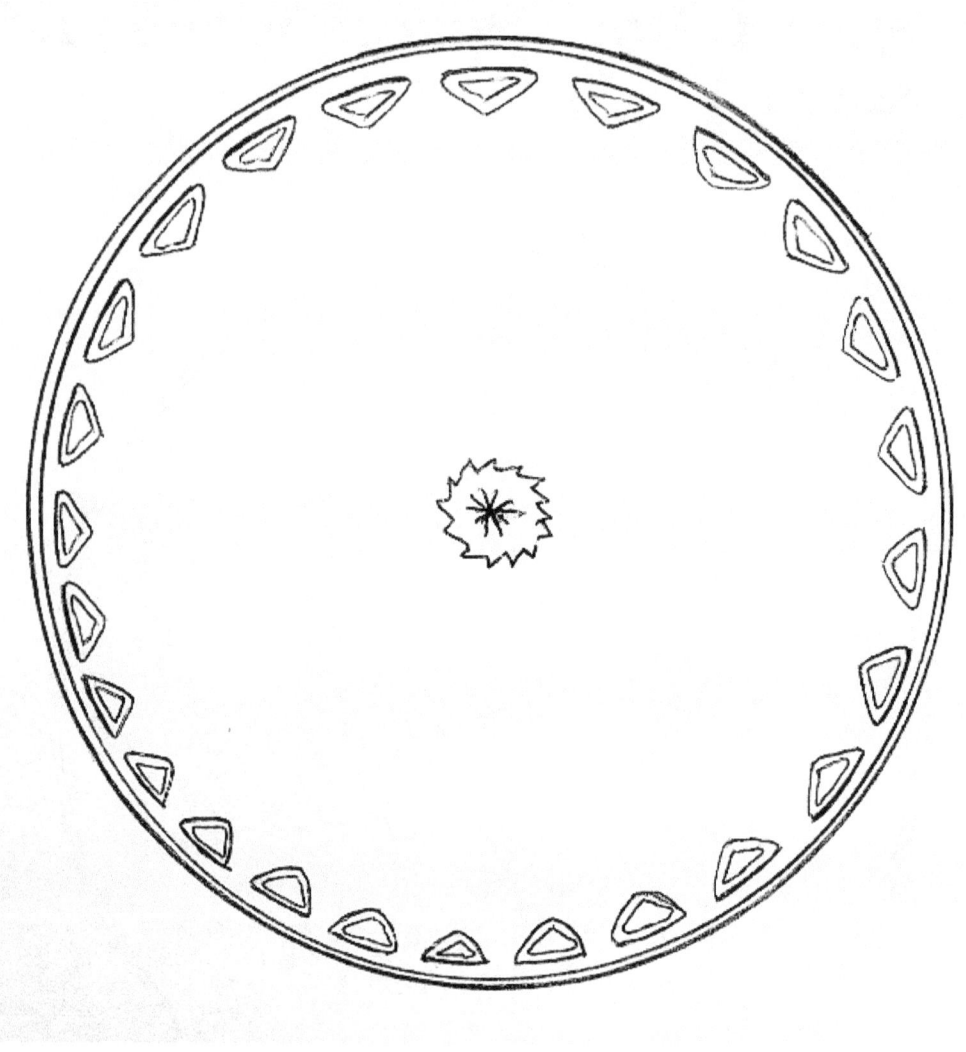

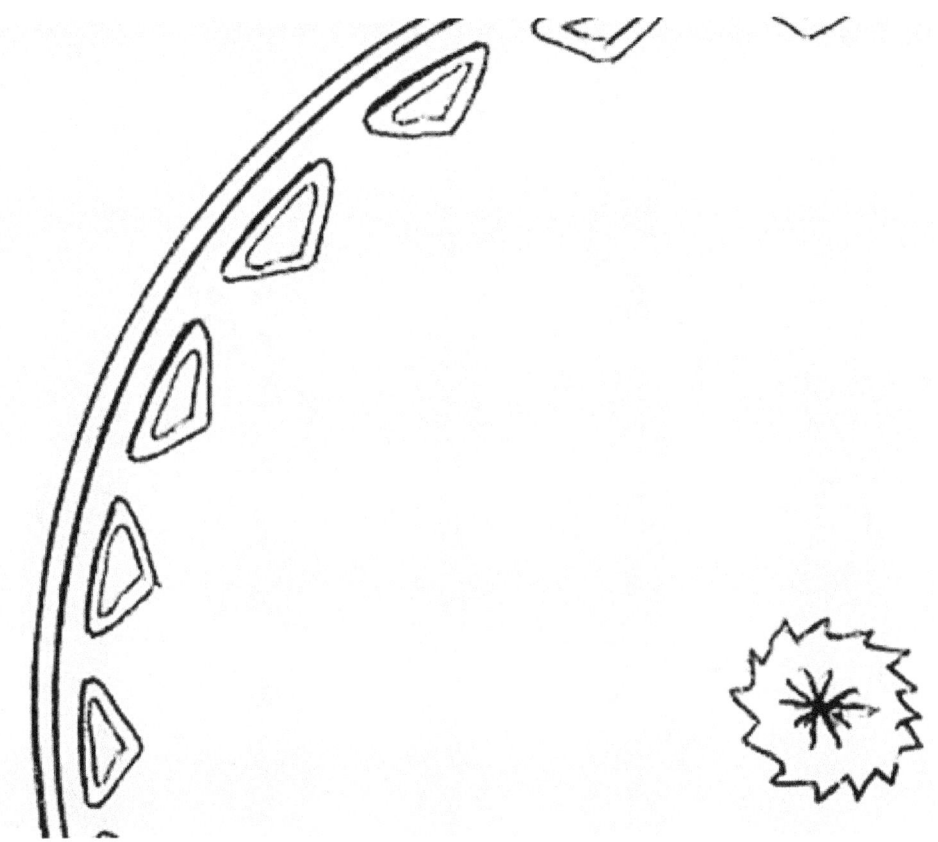

Step 1: Finding Your Center

- Once you draw your outside circle, line it just inside with another circle.

- Using the protractor, find your center point, and draw a small eight-point star to cross the center point.

- Draw small rectangles just inside your outer circle. You don't have to count the triangles, just try to make them all about the same size. Make them a little wider at the bottom.

- Now, line the triangles, but don't fill them in.

Step 2: Filling in the Outside Details

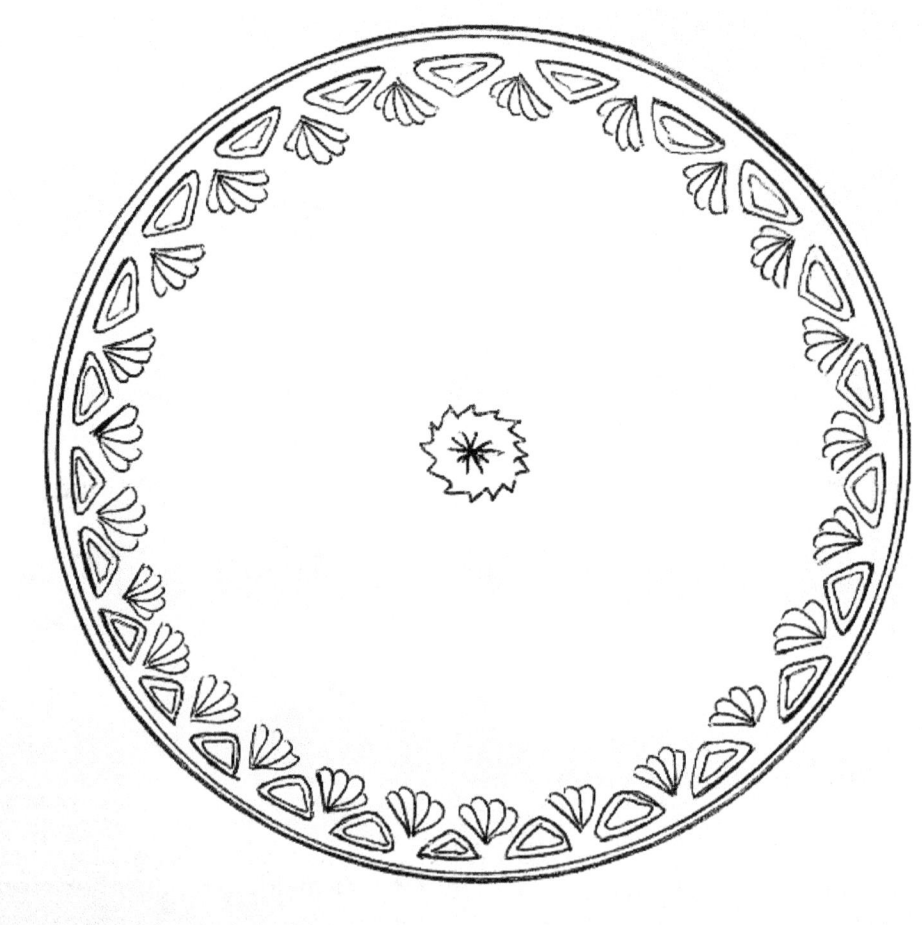

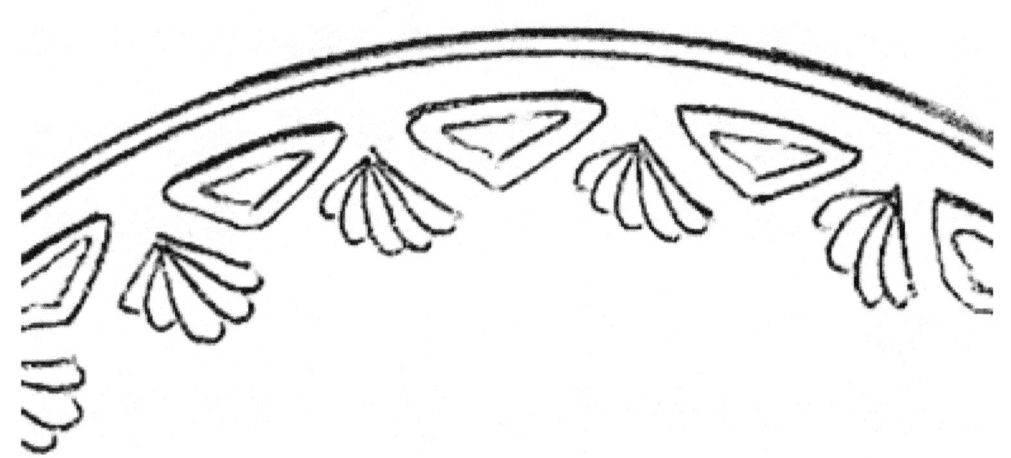

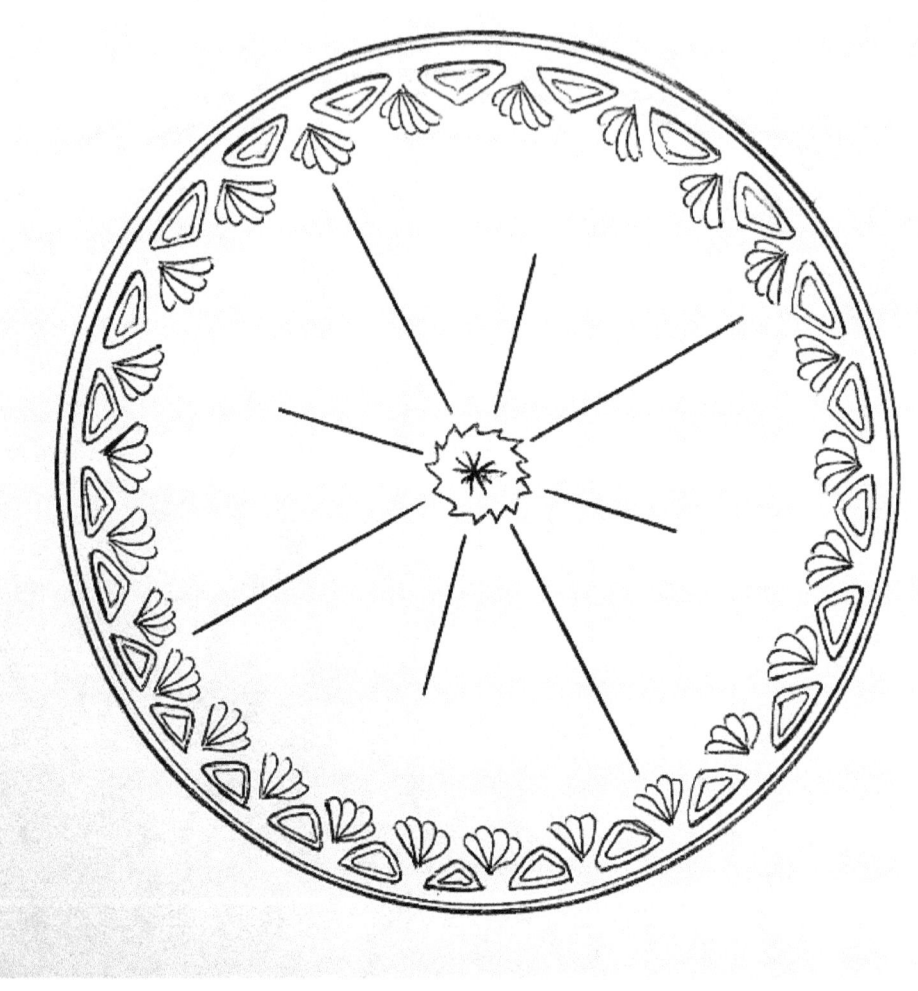

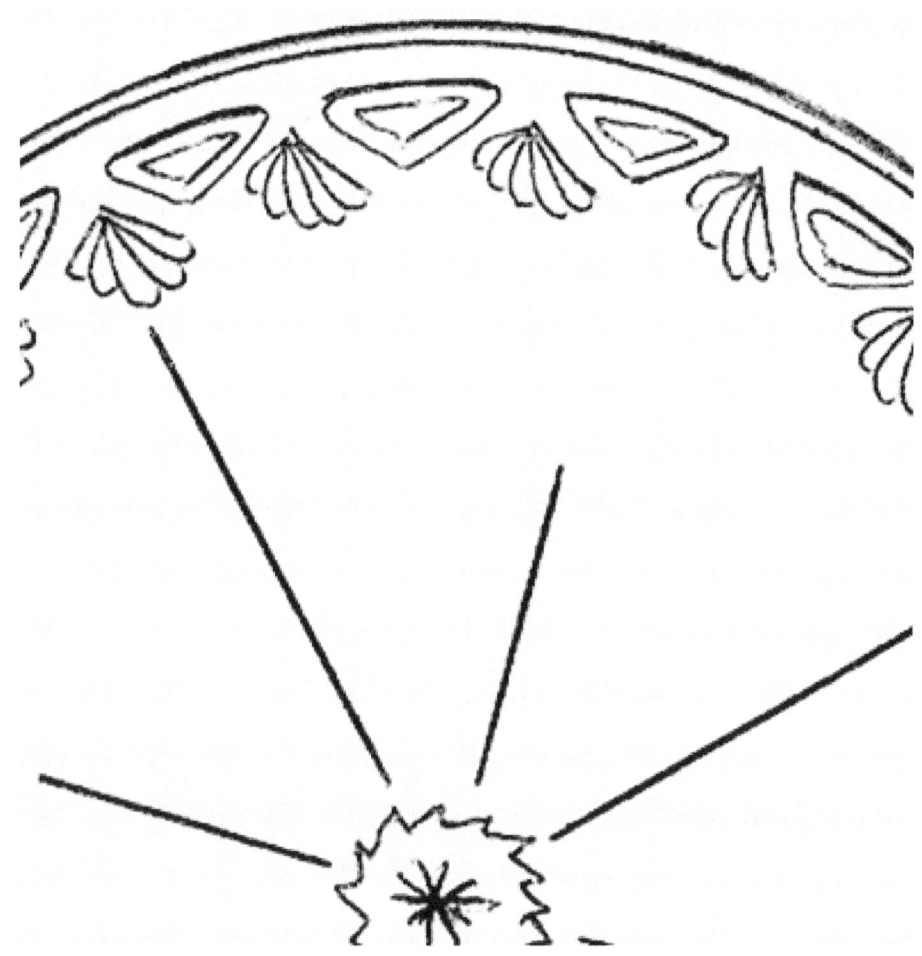

- Design little fans, each one with four parts. Each fan should be placed between the triangles. The fans should be about the same size as the triangles to give the outside edge symmetry.

- Draw a wiggly circle around your center star.

- From outside your wiggly circle, divide your circle in half and then in half again.

- The two main lines that cross should be darker and longer.

- The other two lines should be shorter and lighter.

- Make sure none of these lines touch the wiggly circle or the outer fans. The lines should look as though they are radiating from the center point.

Step 3: Focusing on Your Center Point

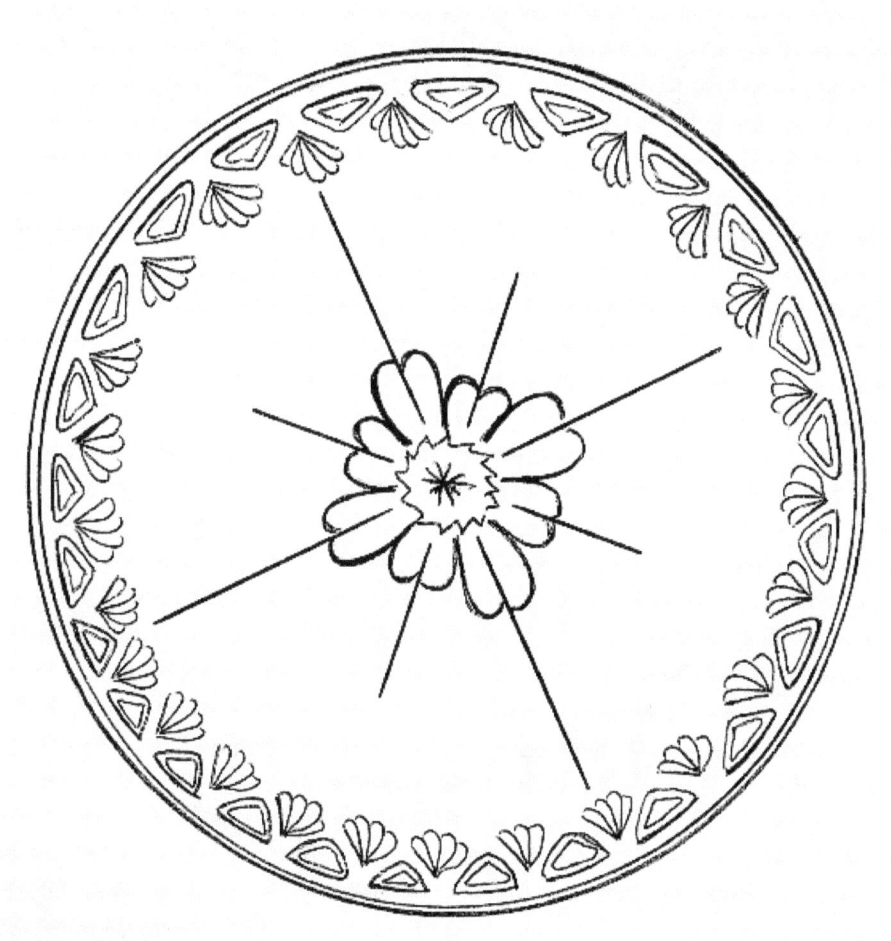

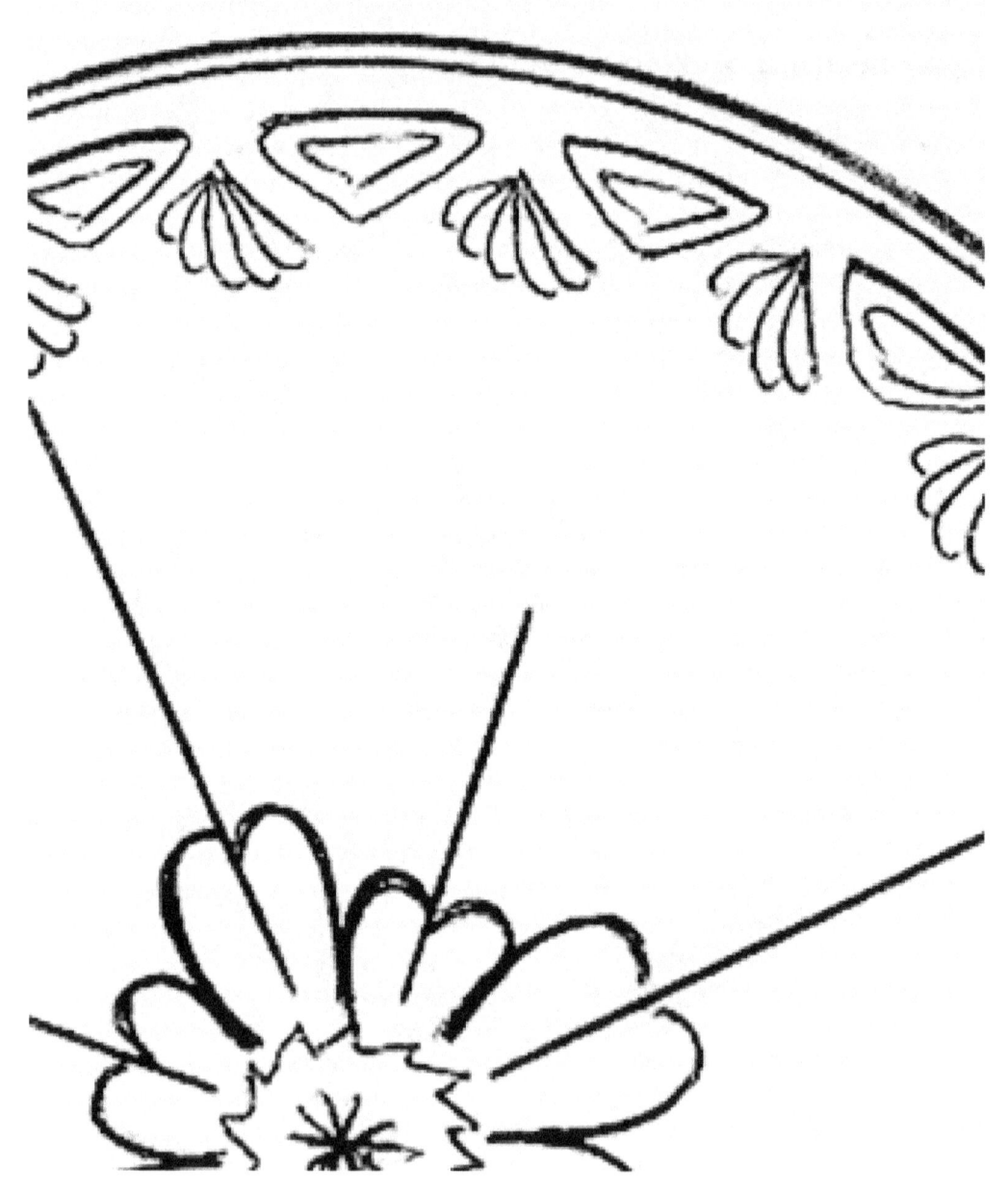

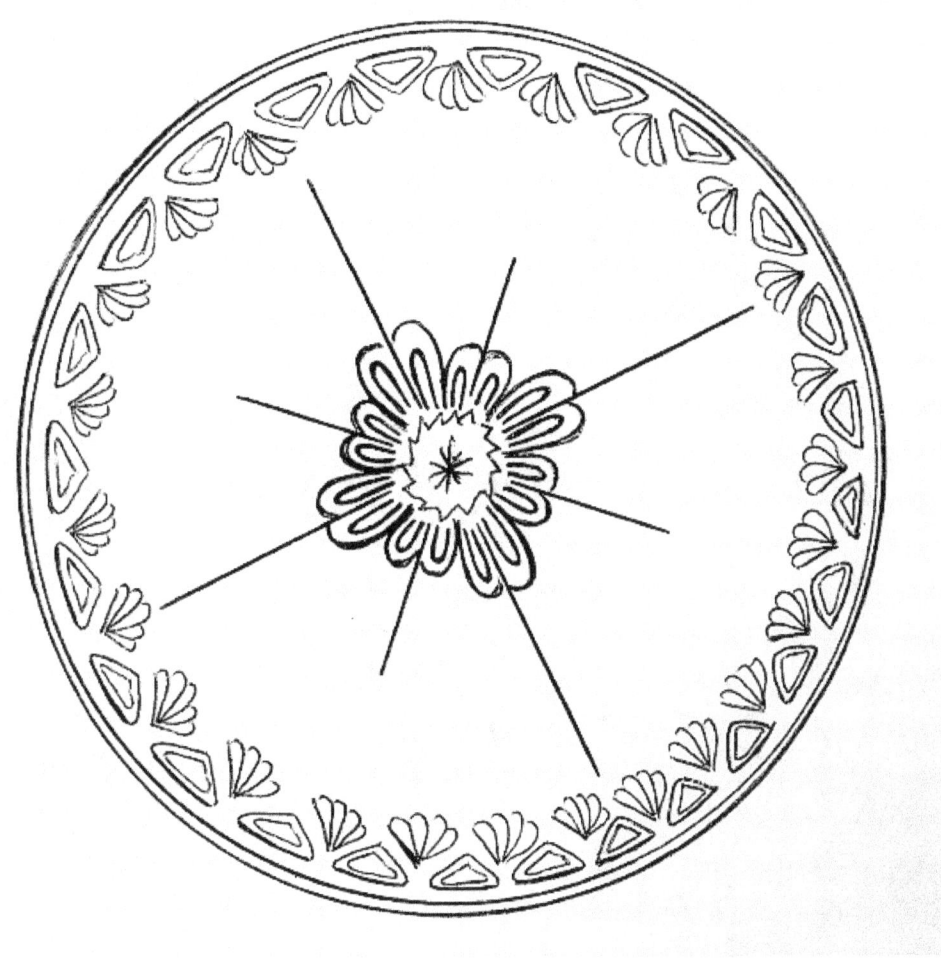

- Just outside the wiggly circle, draw petals. They should be wider at the top then slightly narrow when they get to the bottom. They should appear as an unfinished heart shape.

- Notice how the petals on the longer lines are larger than those on the smaller lines.

- Now draw another loop inside the petals to give detail and dimension.

Step 4: Building Up the Center Point Petals

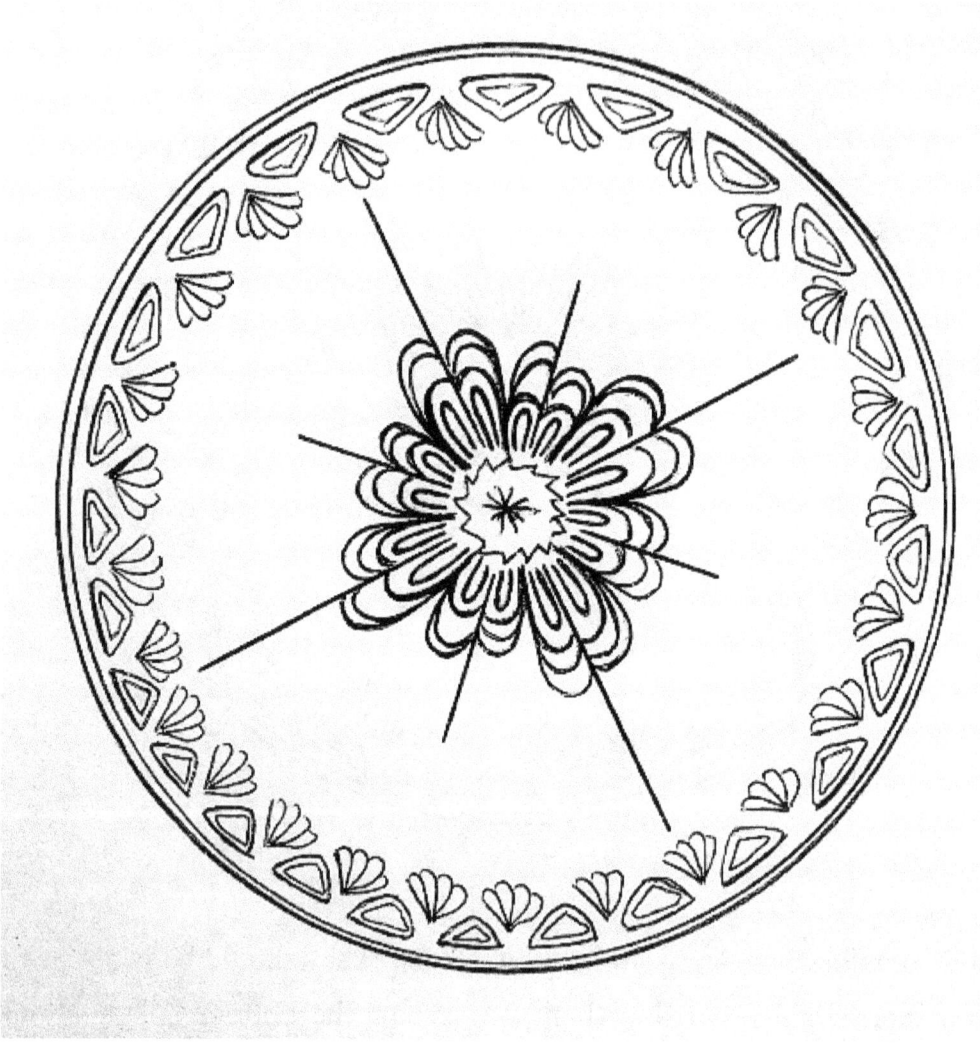

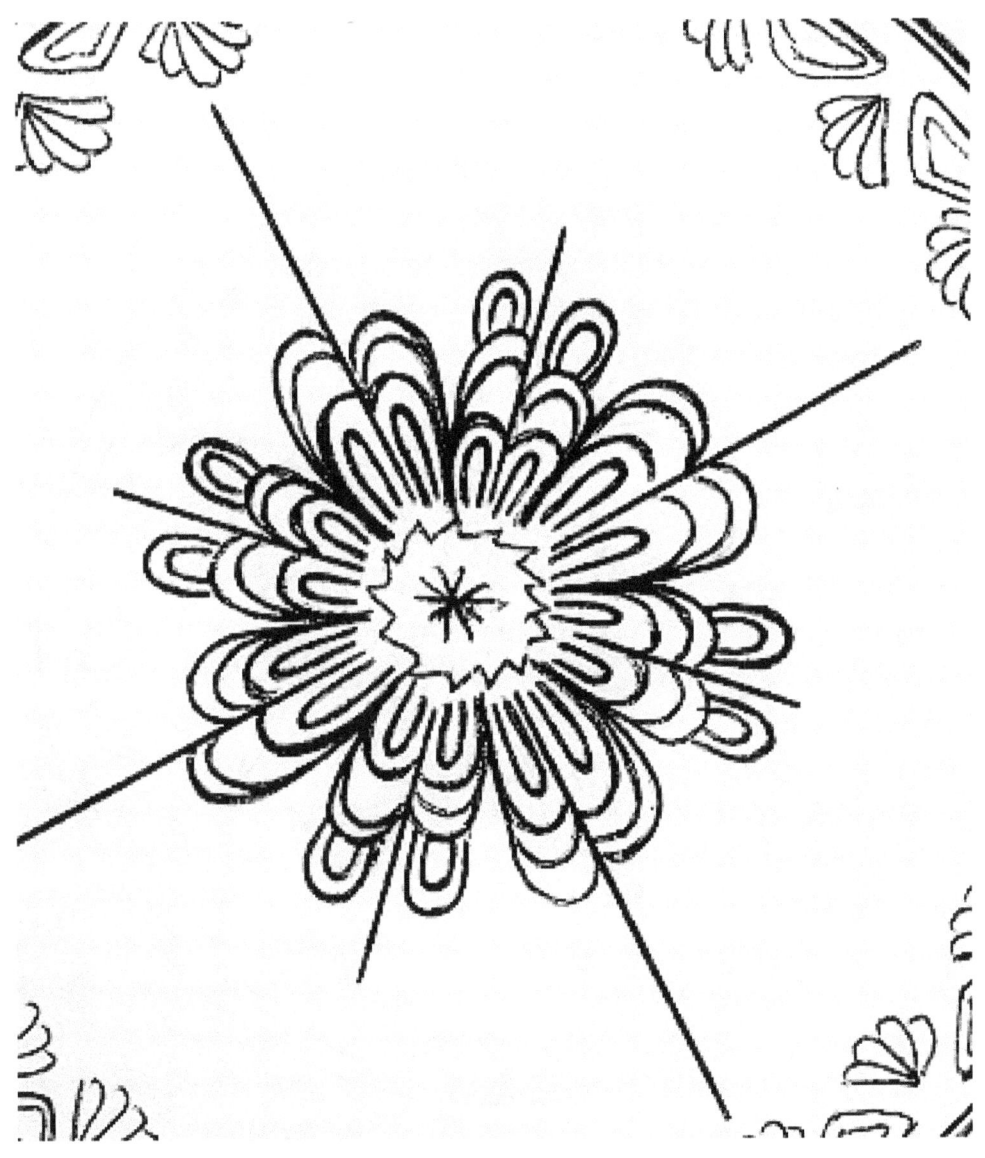

- Layer the outside of the petals by adding two more outlining loops on each petal.

- Notice on the petals on the larger lines, the first outlining loop is longer than the outside petal. On the petals on the shorter lines, the last loop is compressed, making it appear a little elongated. These petals should reach the edge of the shorter lines.

Step 5: Finishing the Mandala

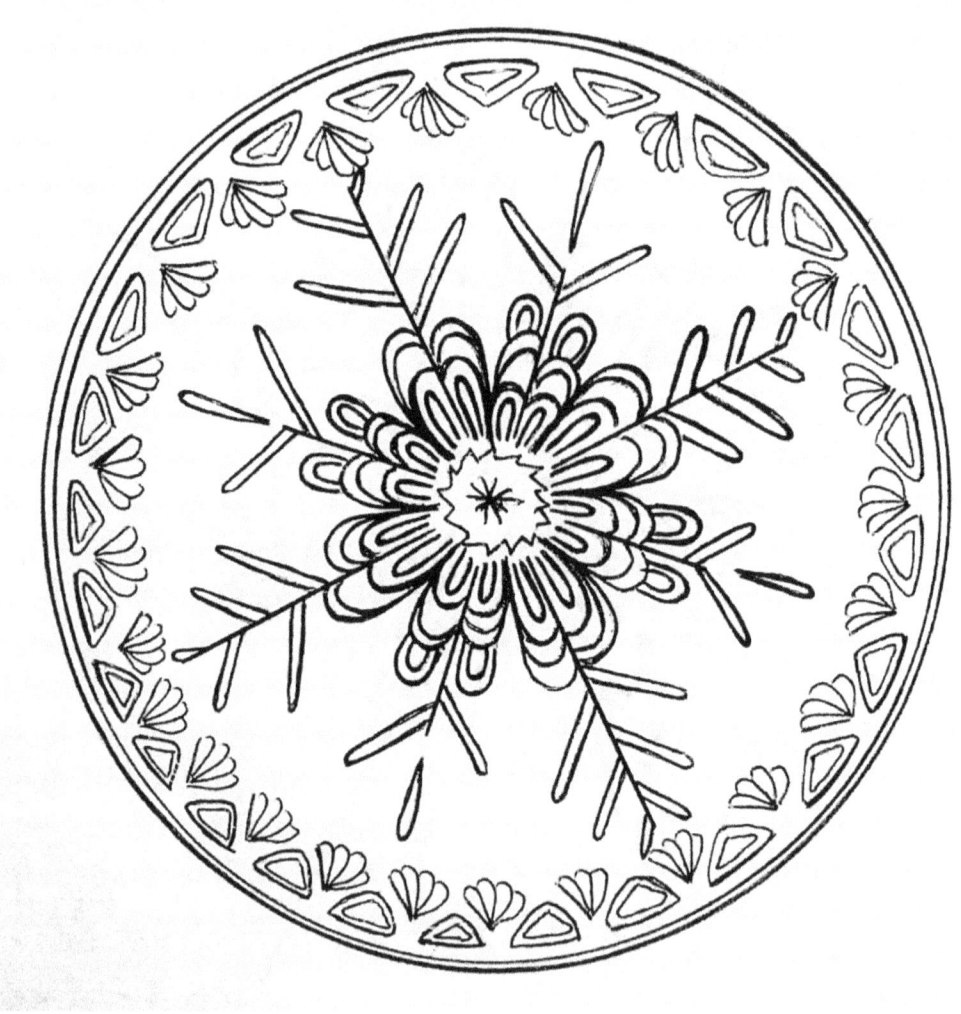

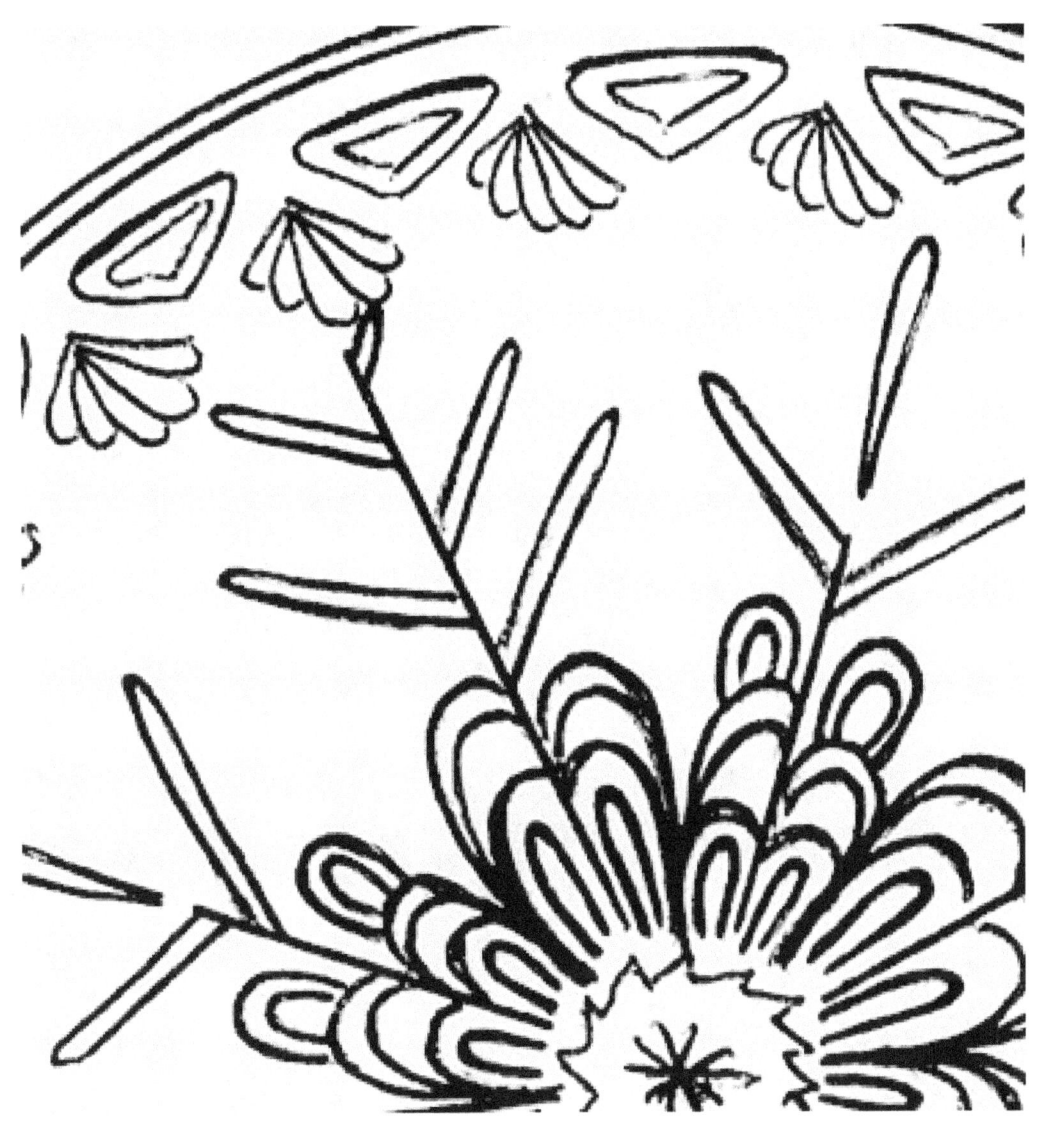

- On the shorter lines radiating from the center point, there should be only three end loops. Notice that the top loop does not touch the radiating line.

- Finish the longer radiating lines by adding elongated loops on them to look like long and narrow leaves.

- Now you have a beautiful, open mandala. This one would be perfect to fill in with color, giving it a bursting effect from the center point.

Chapter 5: The Water Mandala

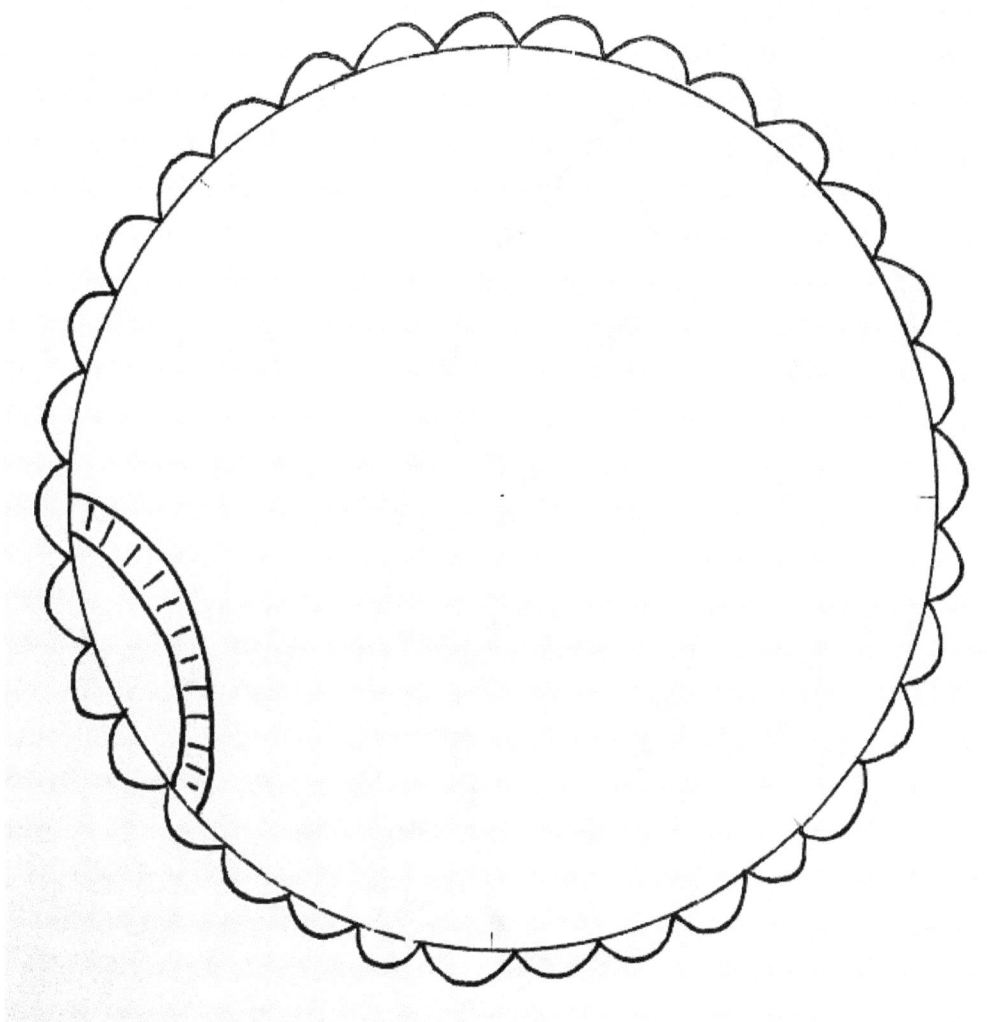

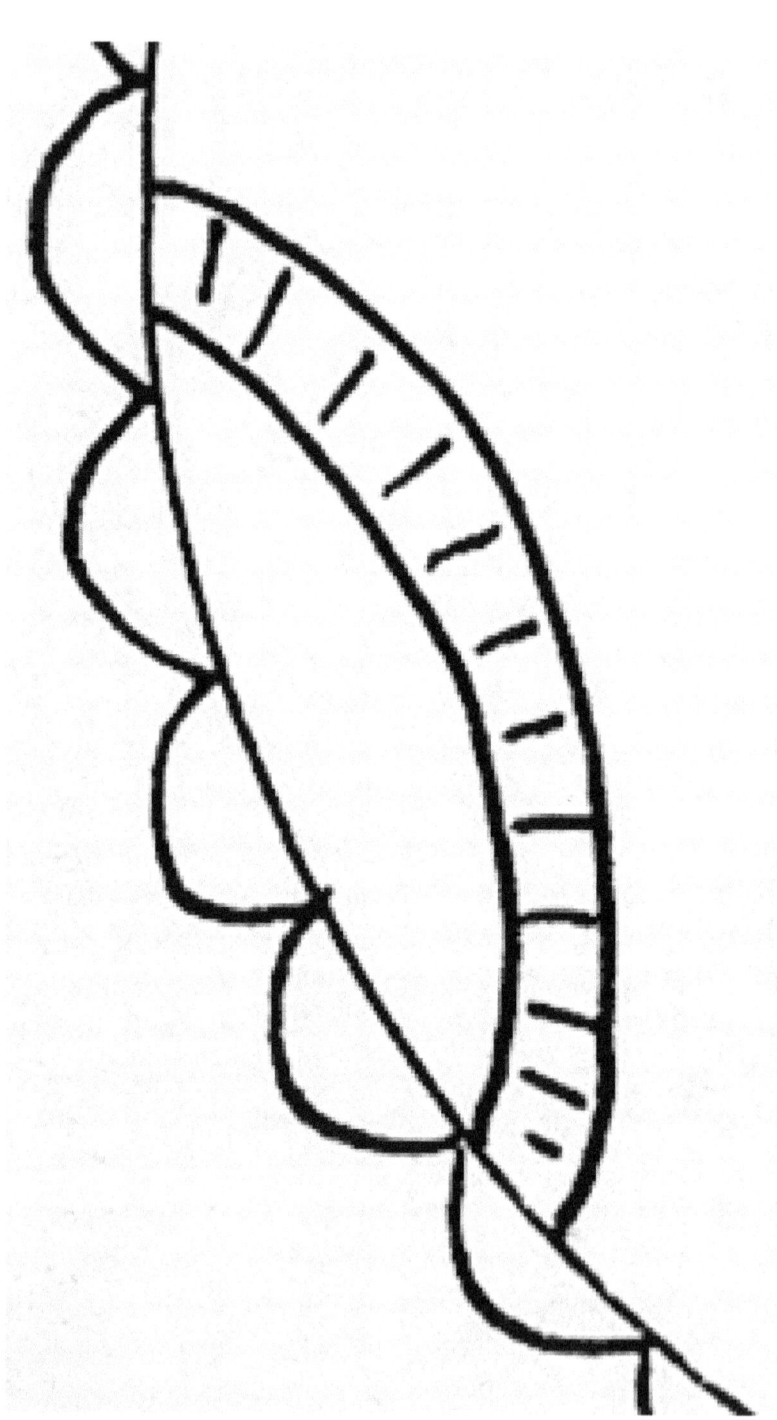

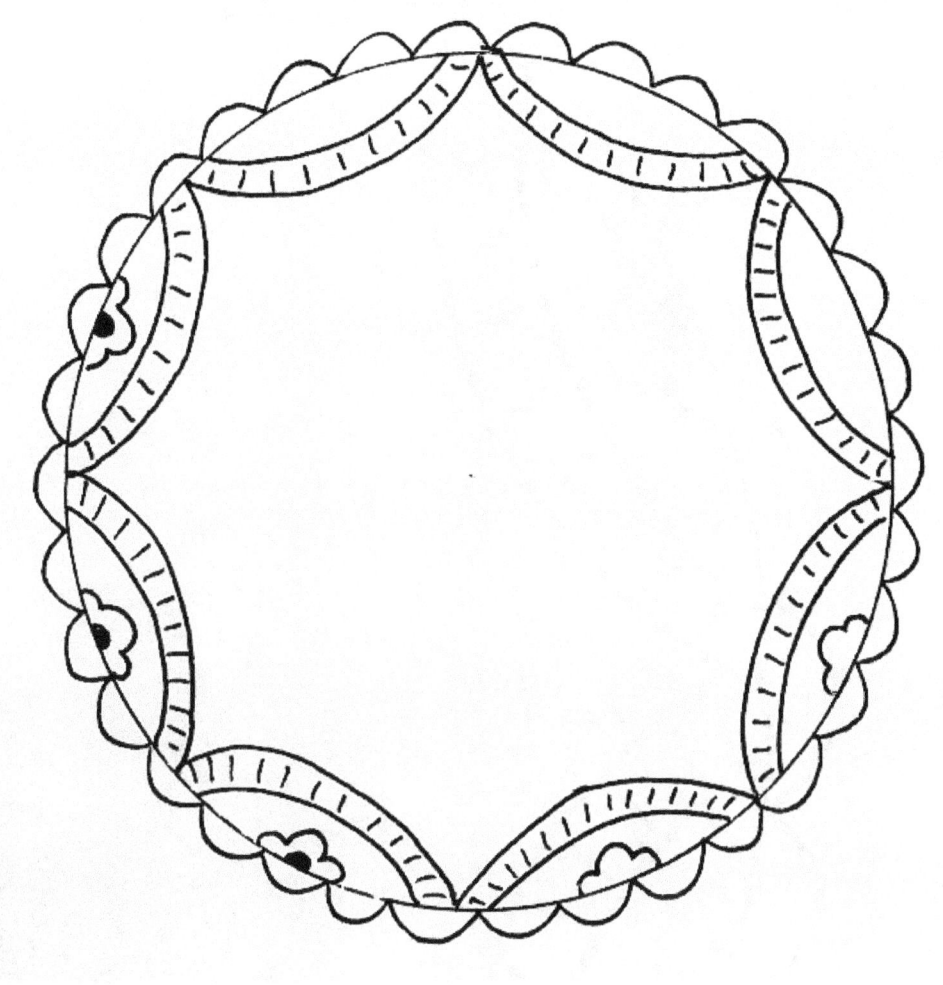

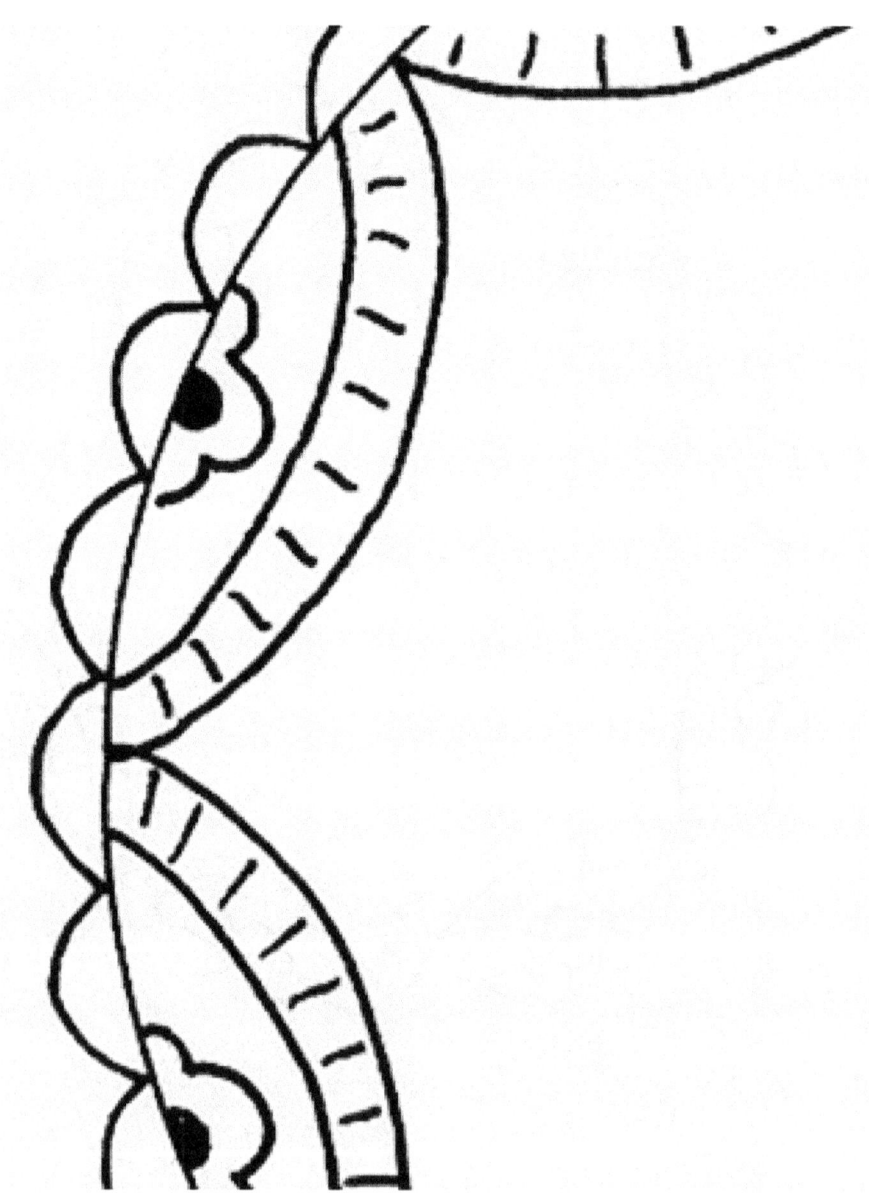

Step 1: Building the Outside Circle

- You'll see soon why we call this our water mandala. Upon finishing, you will see an almost fluid movement in this mandala.

- Once you draw your outside circle, draw lacy loops around the outside edge.

- On the inside of the circle, draw larger loops. Again, try to draw the inside loops about the same size. There should be eight in all. Make it a double loop by outlining the first loop with another line. Keep the thicknesses approximately the same.

- Now add the vertical bars inside the double loop for detail.

- Inside each larger loop, draw a shape that looks like a three-toed paw print with a half-moon dark spot in the middle. Repeat until you have completed the detail around the entire circle.

Step 2: Finding Your Center Point

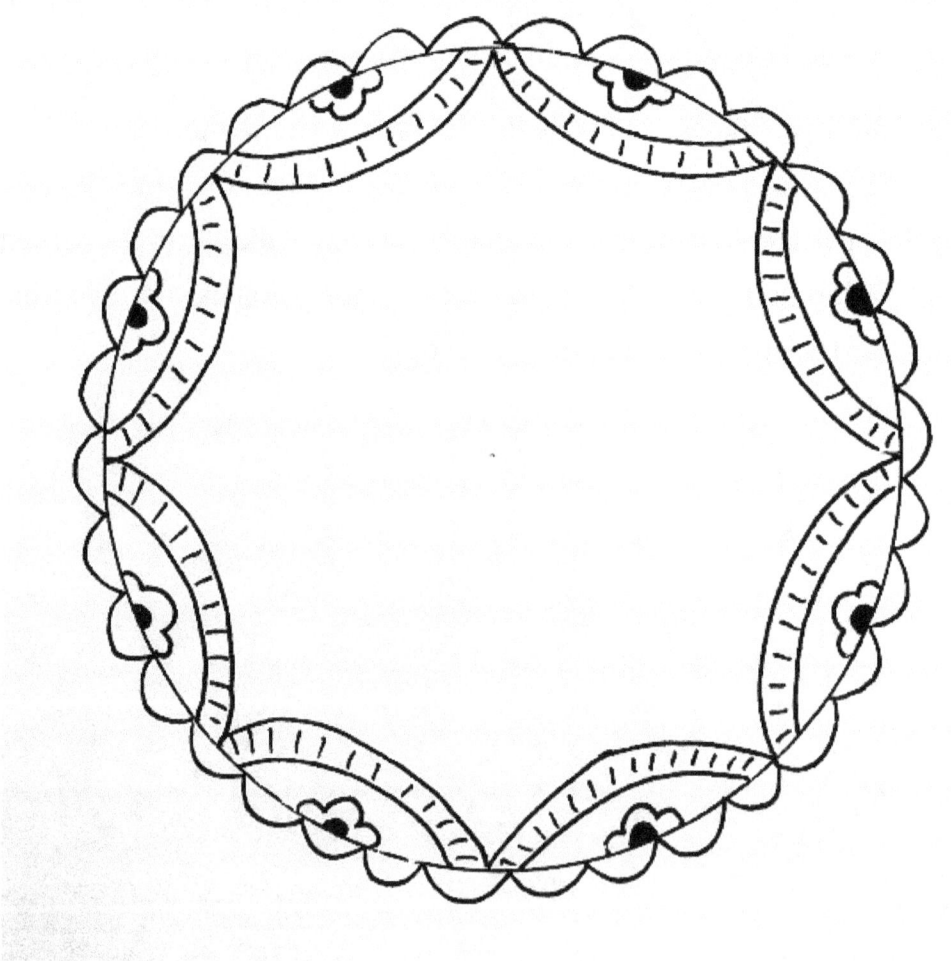

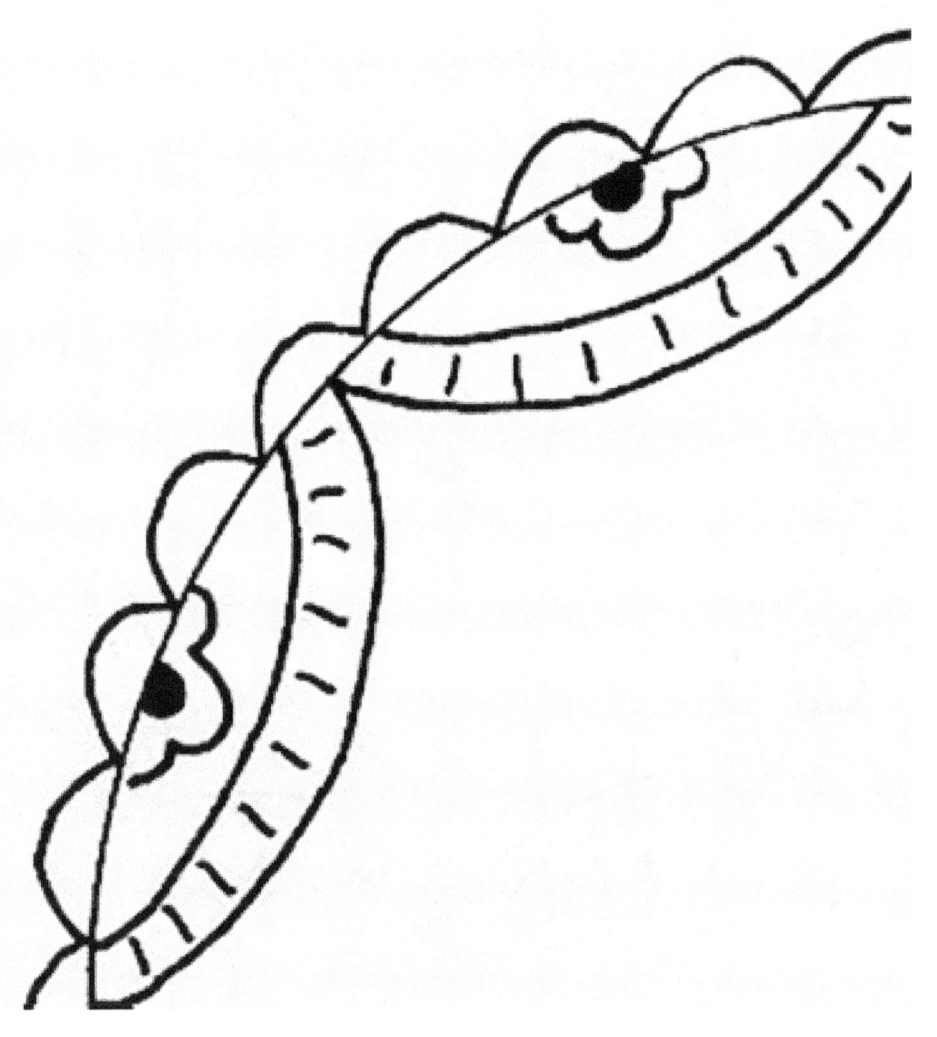

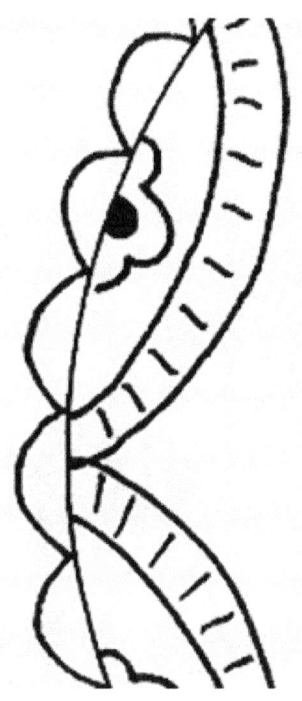

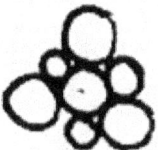

- At your center point, draw an open dot.

- Draw three more open dots, creating a triangular shape. Make sure each of the larger open dots touches the center dot.

- Next, draw three smaller open dots, one to go between each of the larger open dots. Make sure to have all the sides touch. This will give your center point weight and depth.

Step 3: Creating a Fluid Movement

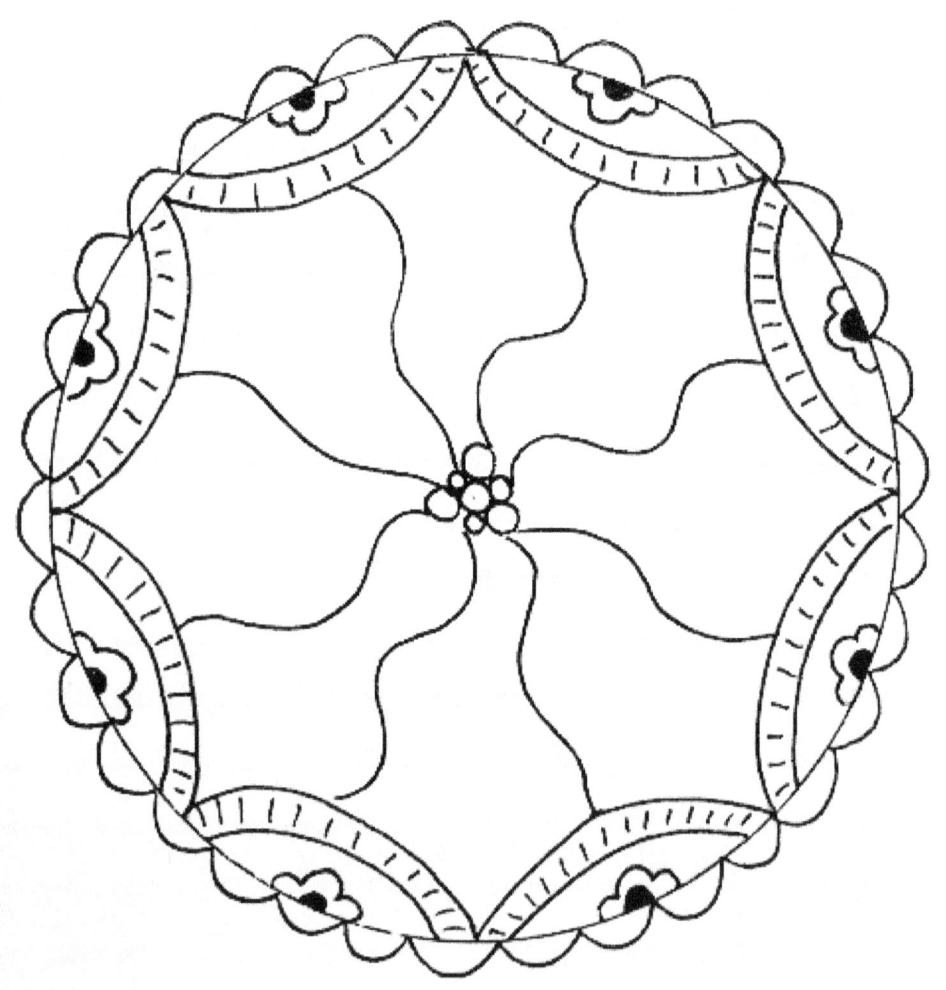

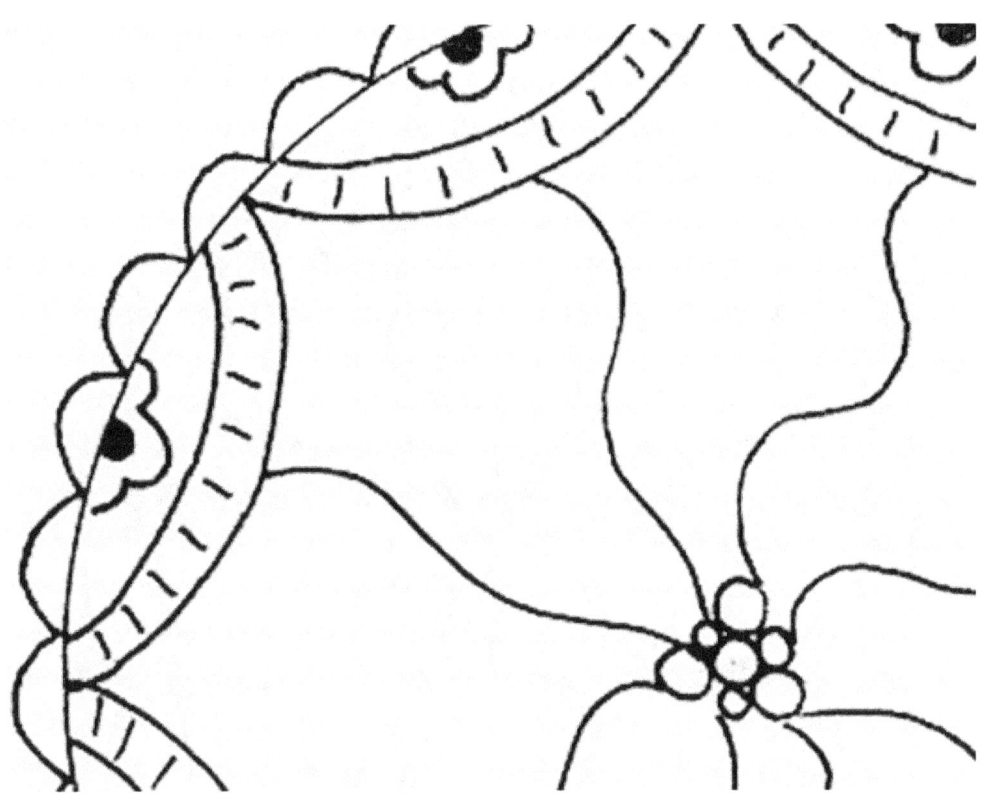

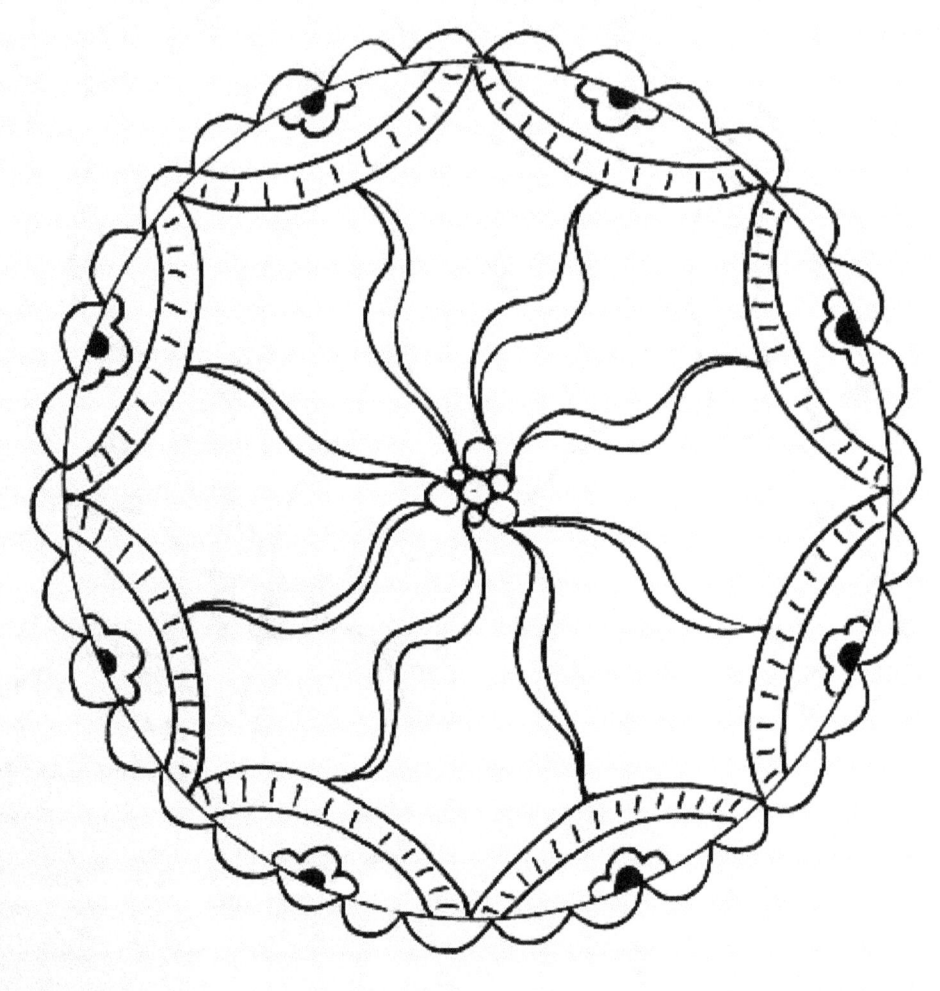

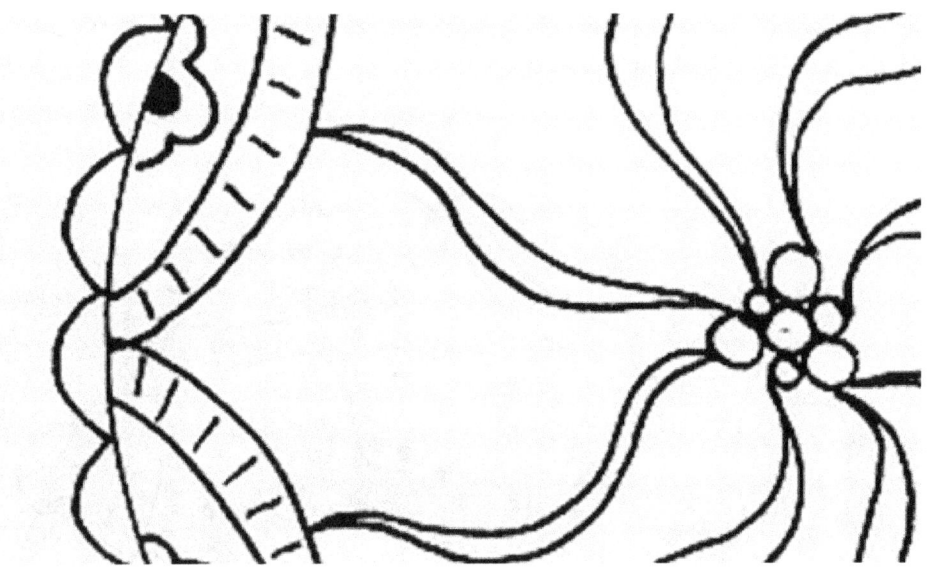

- Here's where the mandala begins to take on the fluid characteristics.

- Draw a large wavy line from each of the large and small open dots to the center of the loops at the circle's edge. There should be eight in total.

- Now, line the wavy lines, making it look like a long leaf.

- Notice each end of the leaf narrow, almost becoming a solid line—creating a thicker center to the leaf.

Step 4: Adding in the Details

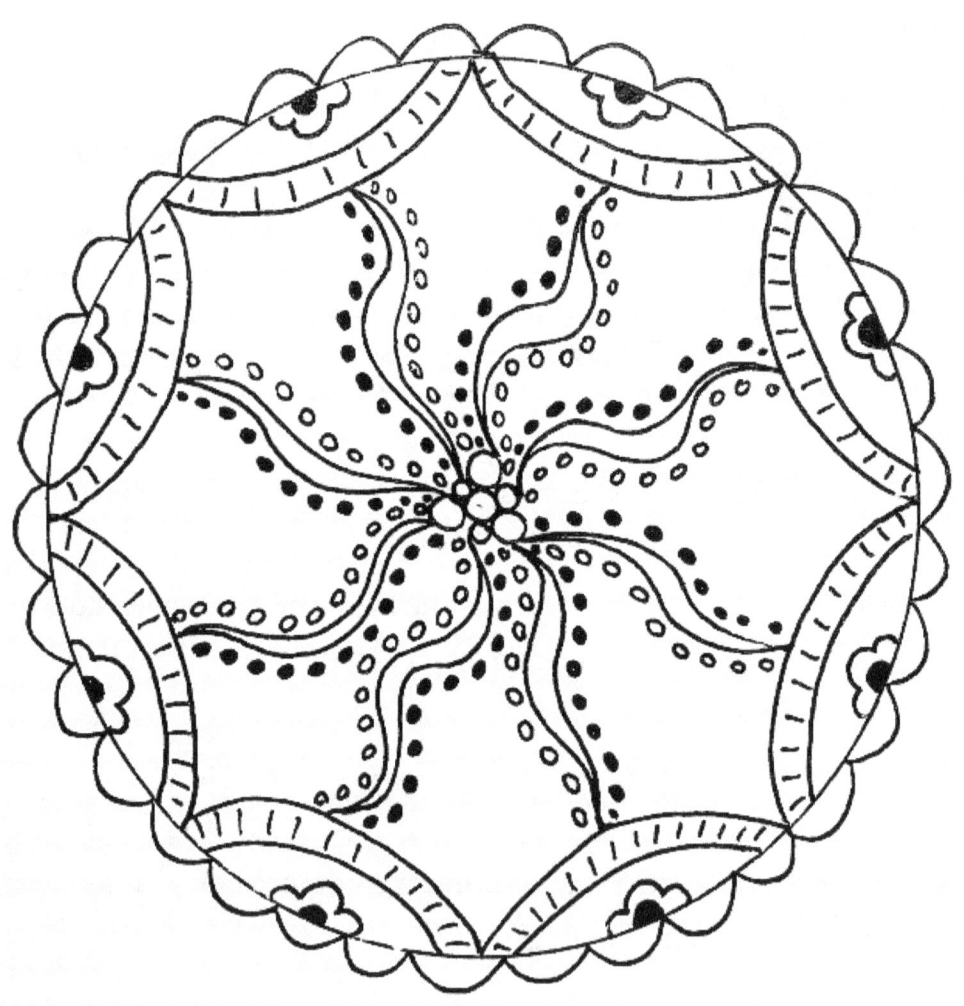

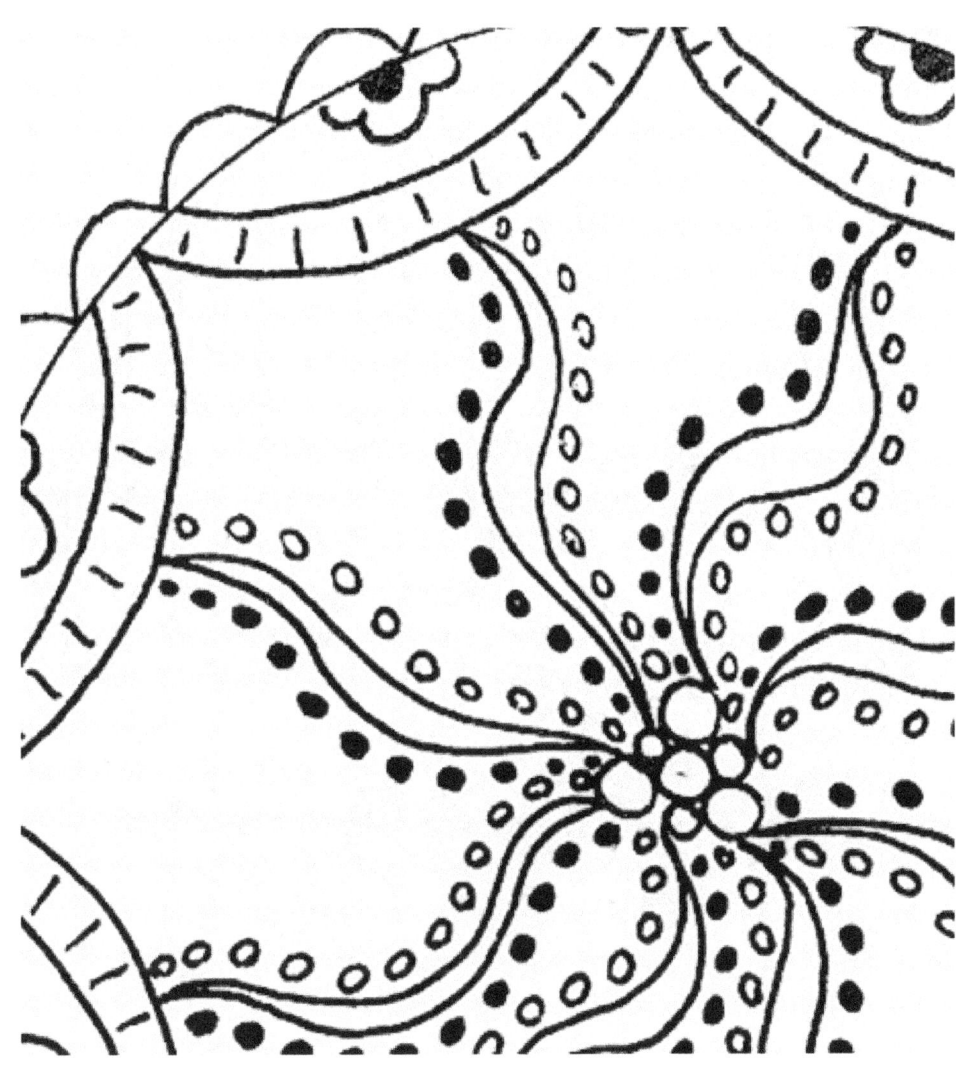

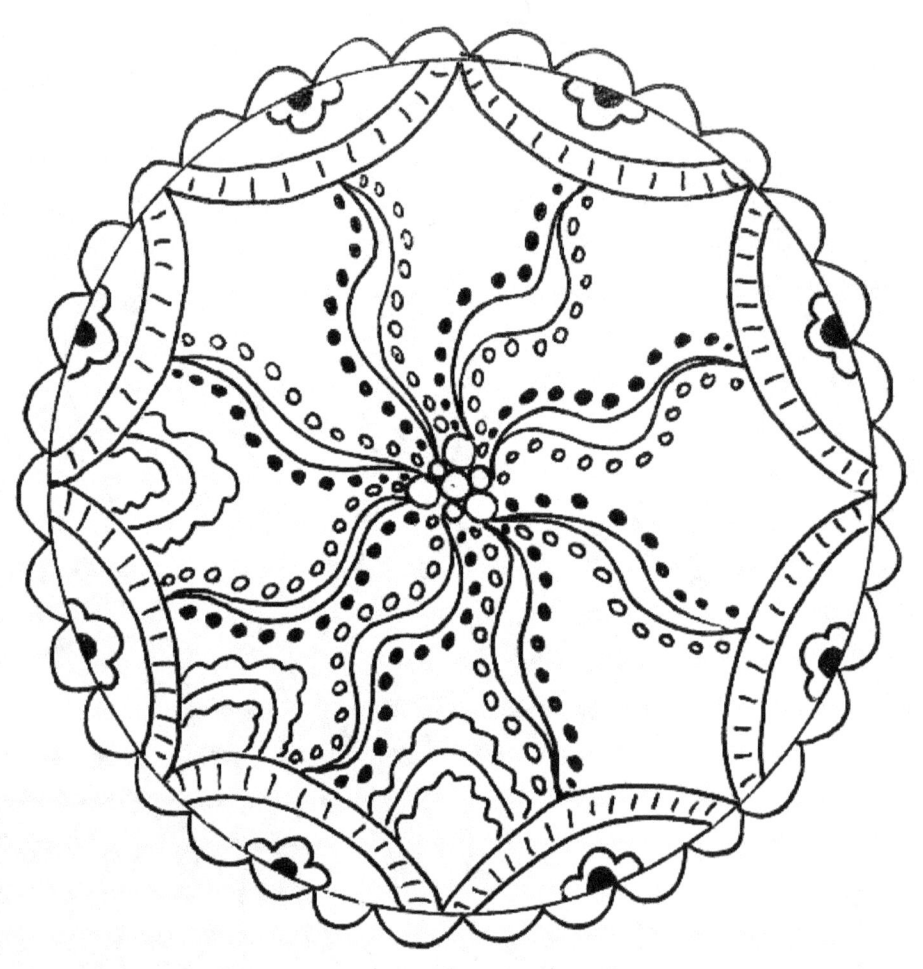

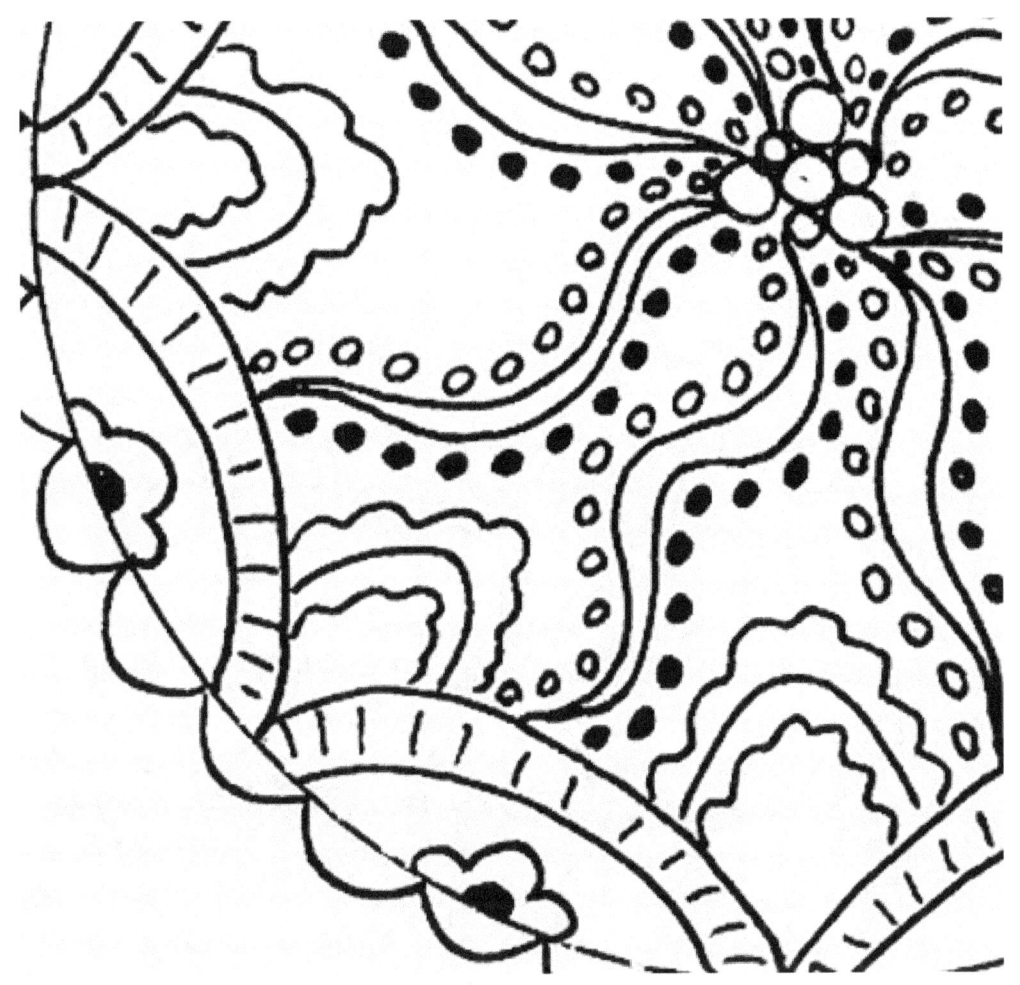

- Now give the inside of the circle some details by adding open dots on each side of the leaves.

- Notice that the dots are filled in on the left side and open on the right side.

- Once you have repeated the pattern all the way around the circle, make the last finishing touch.

- Between each leaf toward the outside of the circle, add a cone. Line the cone on the inside and out with a wiggly line. Your finished mandala will look amazingly fluid as the one below.

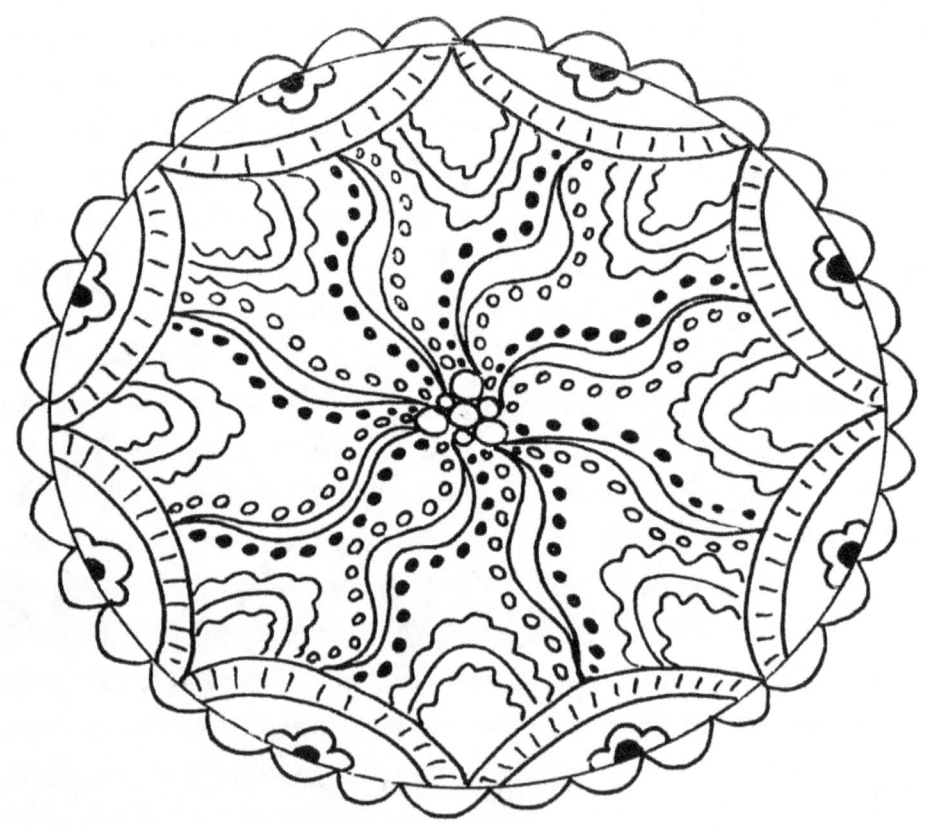

- This is another mandala that would look wonderful colored in blues and greens.

Chapter 6: Practicing a DIY Mandala

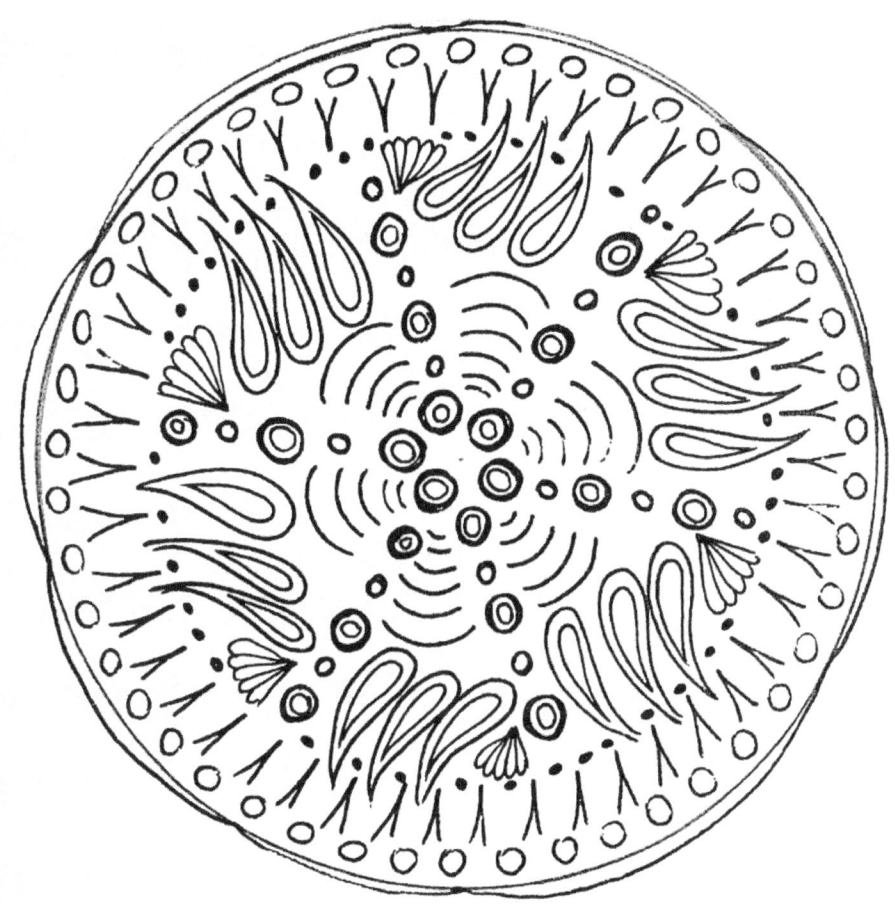

Step 1: What Would You Do First?

- _____

  _____

- _____

  _____

- _____

_____

Step 2: Let's See How You Did

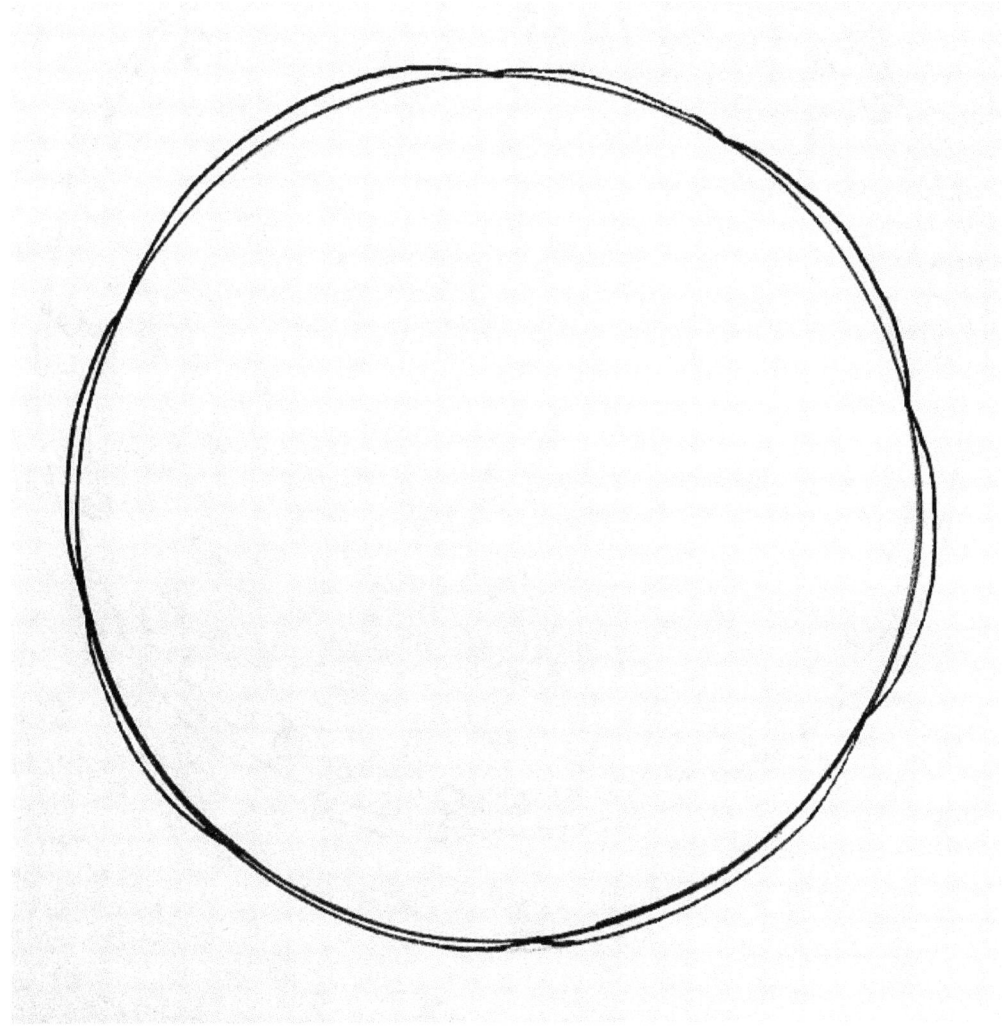

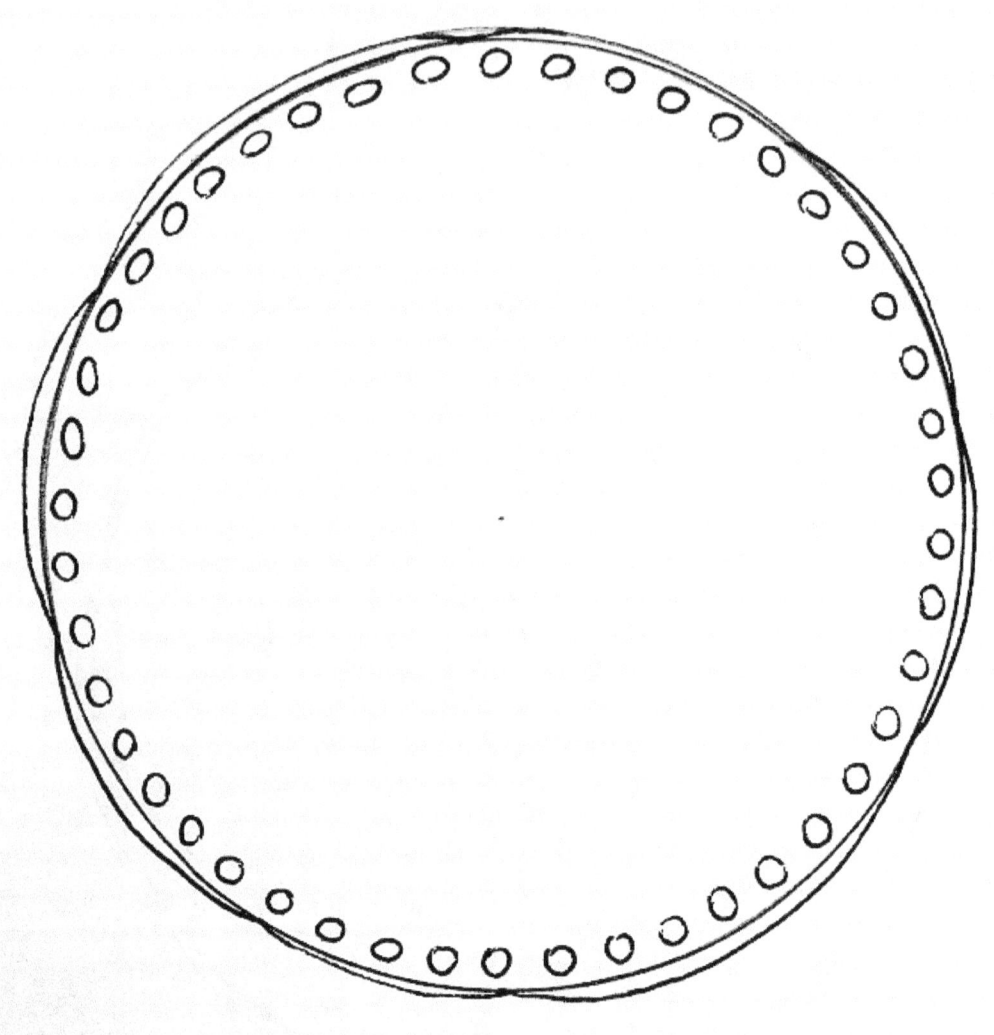

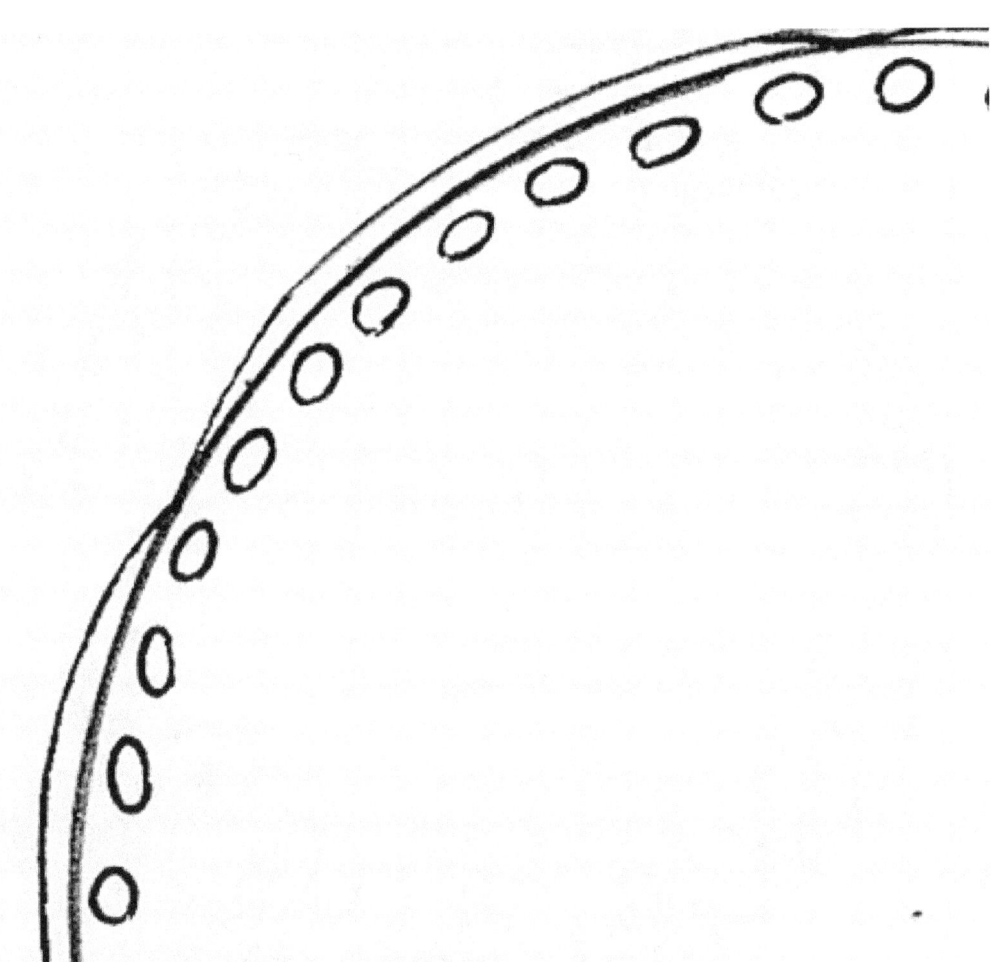

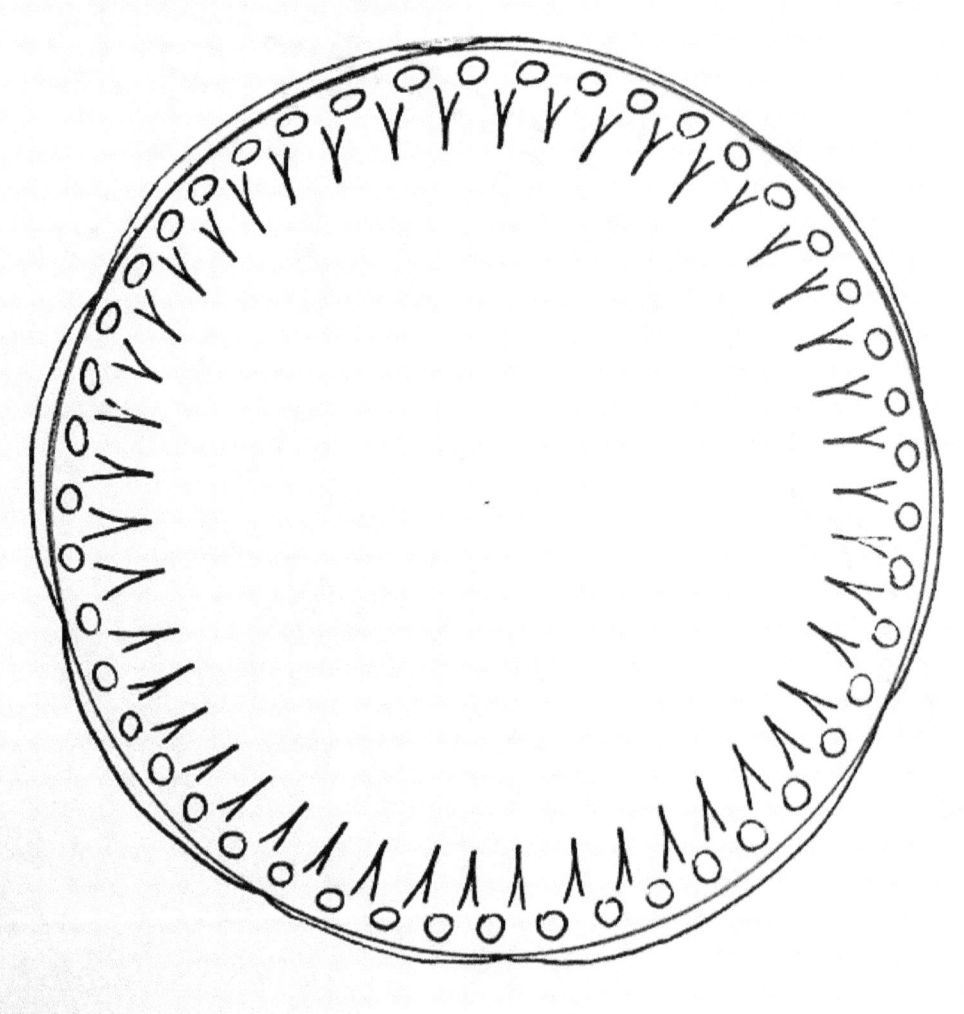

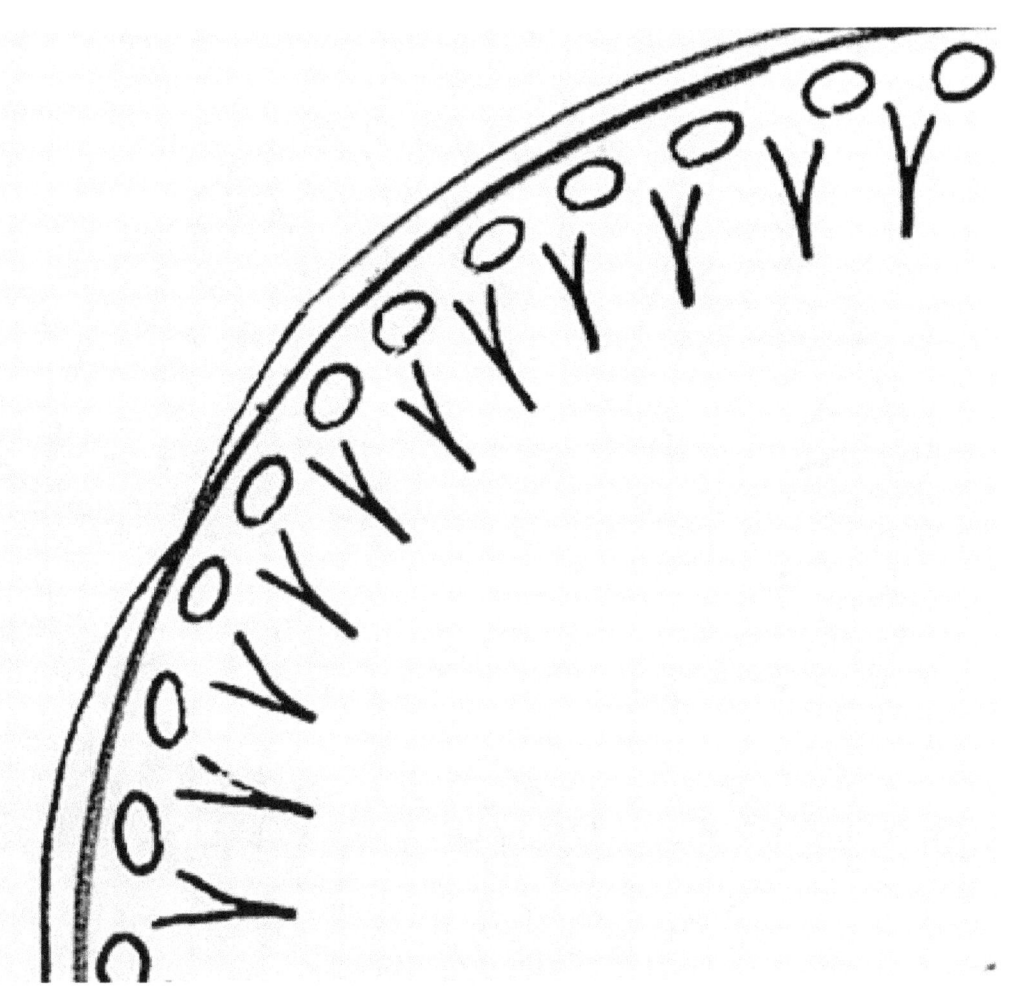

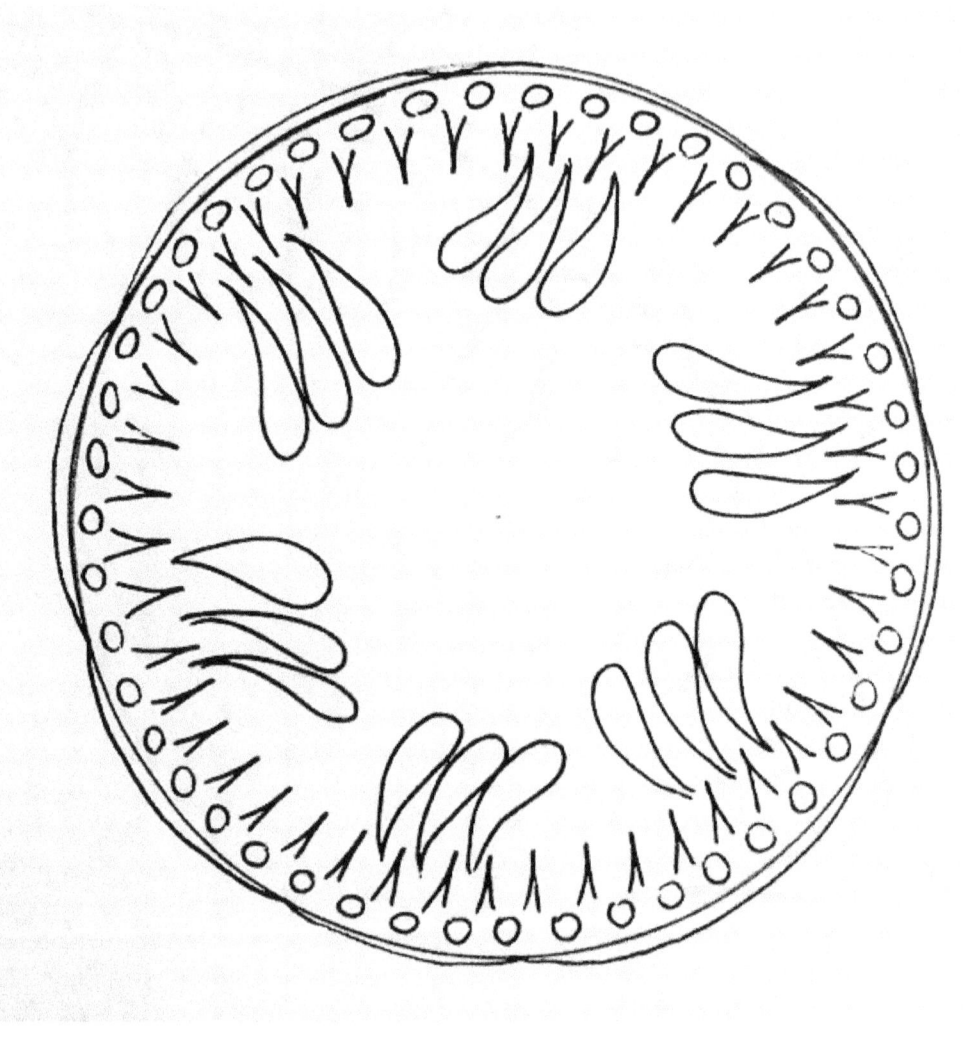

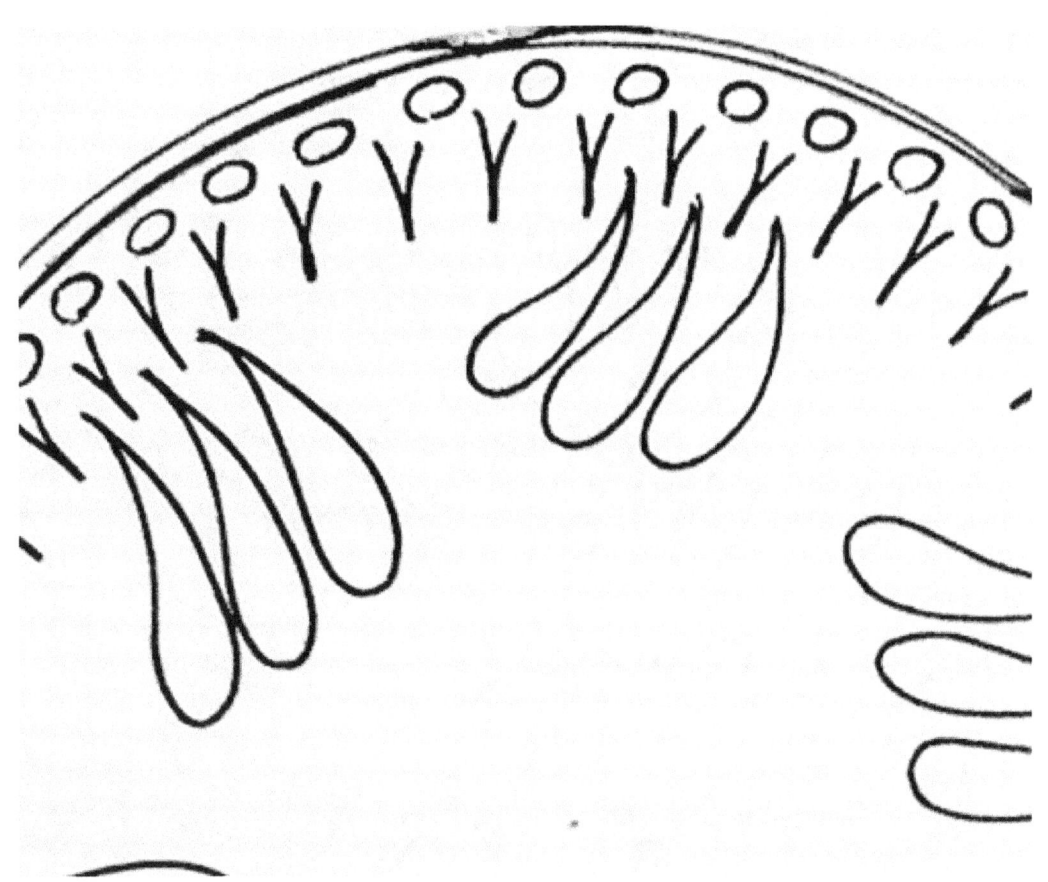

Step 2: Adding the Details

- Are you paying attention to the details?

- Did you find your center line?

- Does your mandala look balanced so far? If not, what did you do wrong?

Step 3: More Details to Fill in the White Space

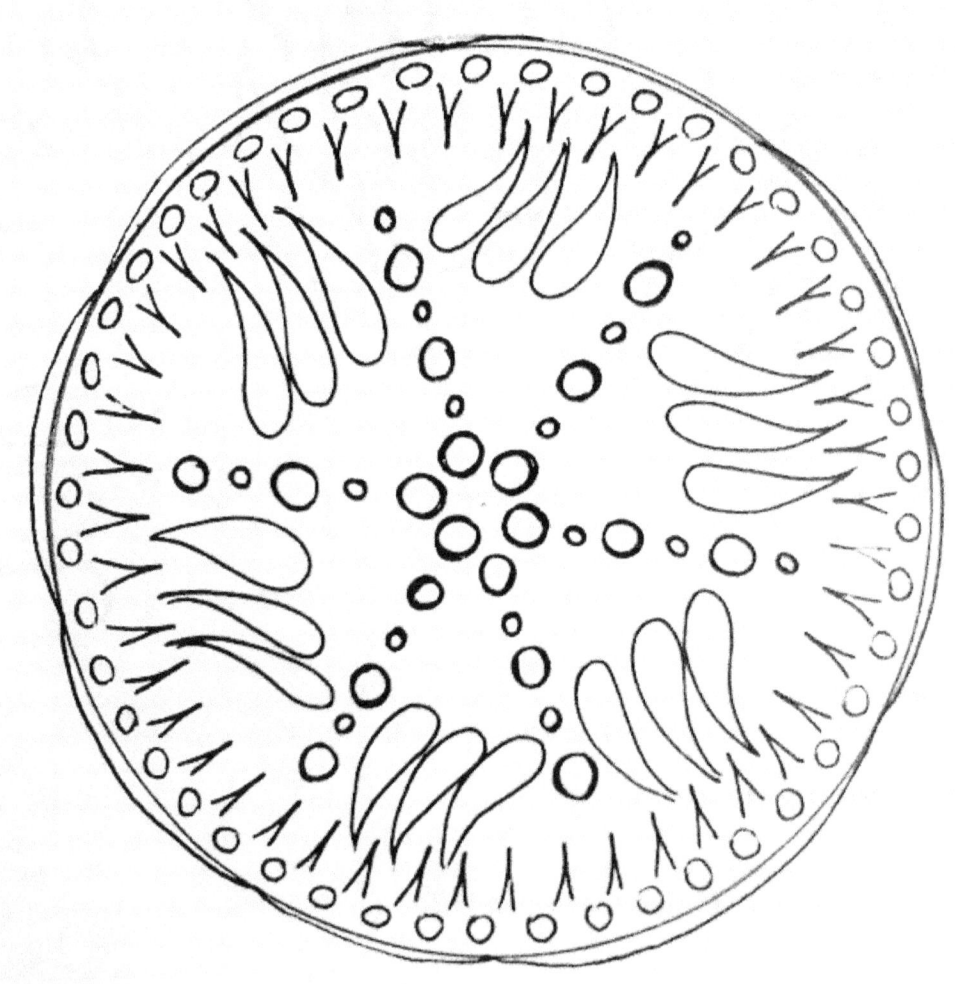

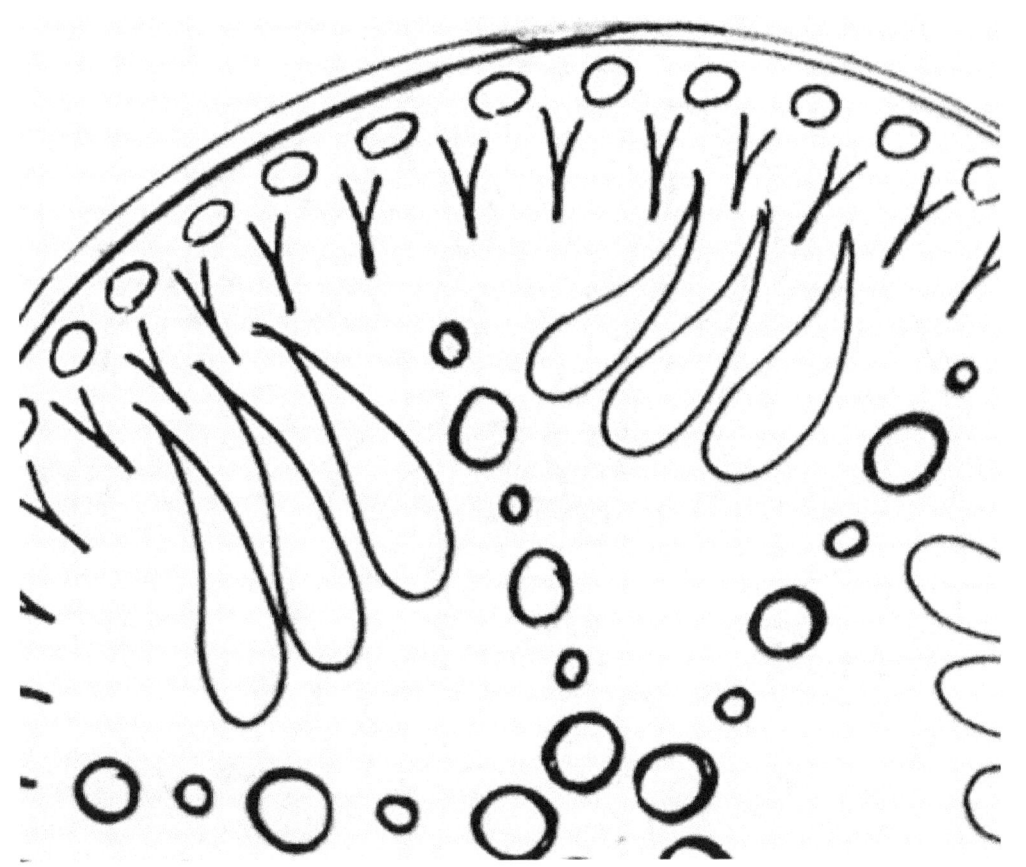

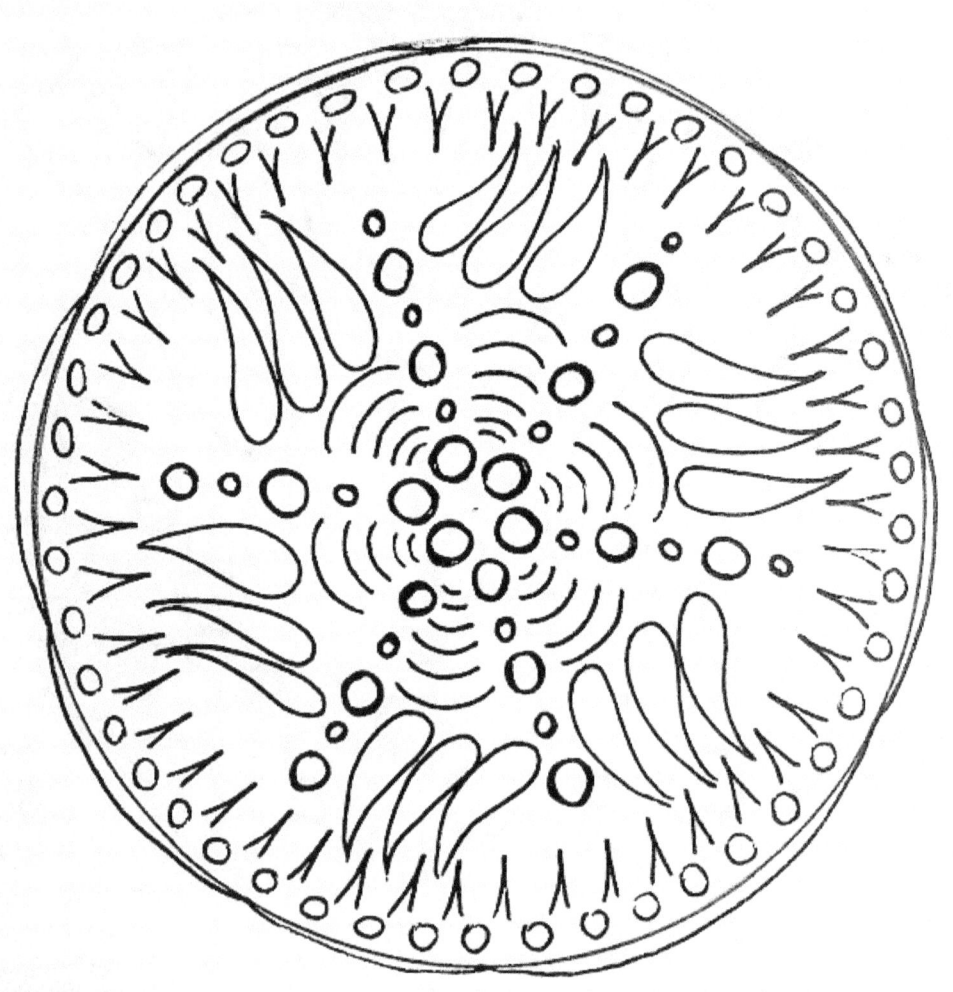

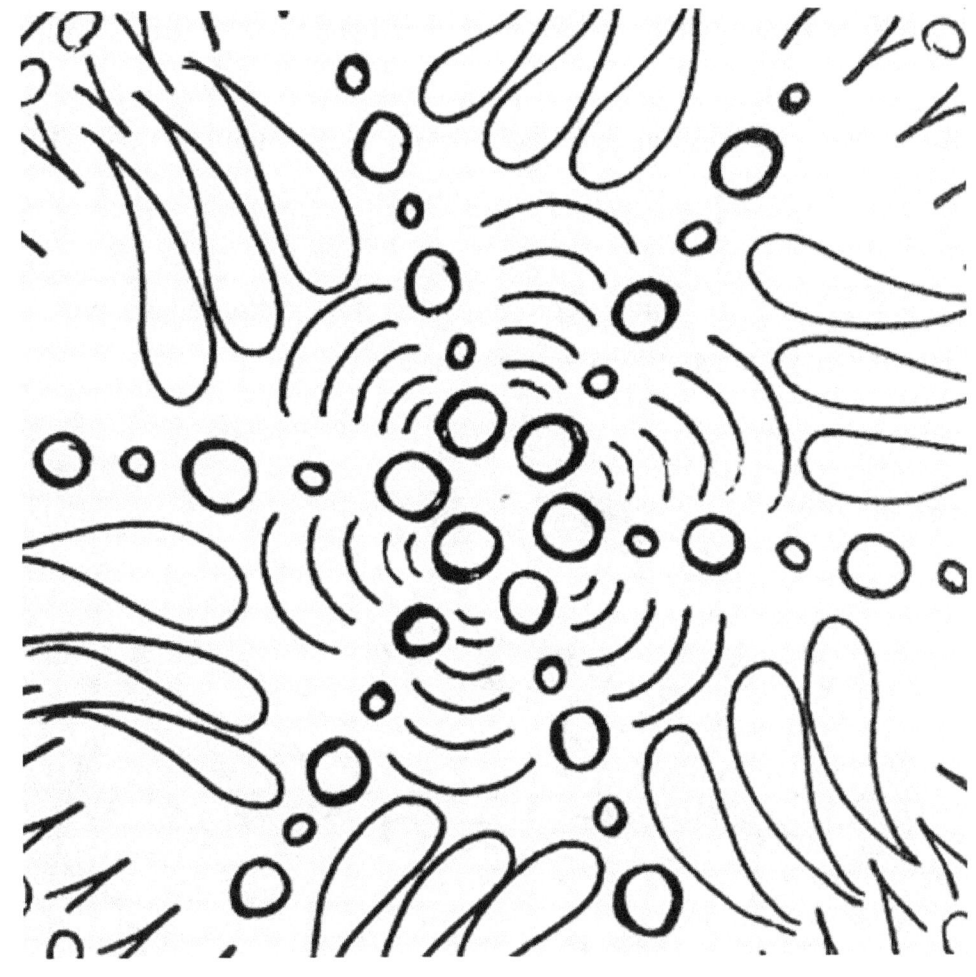

- Can you see how adding more details to your mandala makes it eye-catching and interesting?

- Step back and compare your mandala with the sample we have provided. Have you created balance?

- What should you have done differently?

Step 4: Finished—Now Add Your Own Signature to the Mandala

- Either change something or add something to the mandala to give it your own signature—your own special touch.

- Color it or fill it in to add depth and weight. Create new shapes if you like, but use your artistic eye to make it your own.

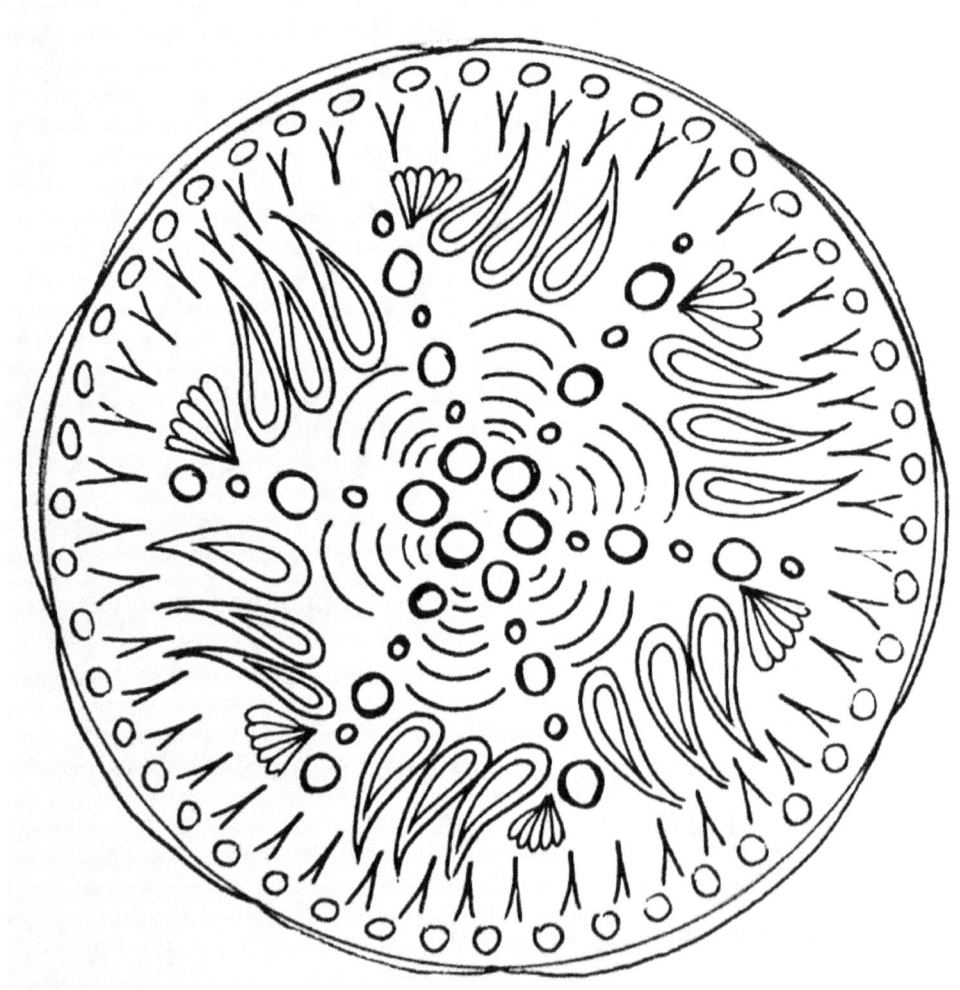

Conclusion:

Thank you for drawing mandalas with me today, and for creating your own at the end. I hope you are encouraged to get creative and have fun by creating a whole notebook of mandalas. Don't be shy about using shapes and colors that are imaginative and make your work enjoyable for you and entertaining for people who view your art.

The next step is to practice. If your mandalas were somewhat imbalanced, practice will help to correct that issue. If you are sitting at home, grab a sheet of paper and draw a mandala freehand, using unique shapes and sizes, colors and angles to create a relaxing and fun experience. The fun of drawing mandalas is that there is no right or wrong way, just let your imagination take charge and have a good time. Think positively and let your mandala express your feelings in the moment.

Here's a challenge, create a mandala every day for the next ten days. Then, compare the difference in each one. With every mandala, you should see greater detail and more balance. Many artists enjoy mandalas so much, they weave them into images, rugs, and put them on dishes or mugs. Mandalas can be intricate or whimsical, mysterious or fluid. They can reveal your moods and feelings, and deliver a time of relaxation and meditation as you draw them.

I hope you experiment with mandalas, and you are encouraged to expand the shapes and sizes you draw. Finally, if you found this book useful and fun, please write a review on Amazon and encourage others to join in the fun of drawing mandalas. Your feedback is always appreciated.

Thank you!

Thank you for choosing our book, we hope you found it interesting and helpful.

If you liked the book, please give us a favor to write your review.

We would really appreciate this!

If you would like to have a bonus – **FREE BOOK**, please send the screenshot of your review to this e-mail:

kelly.artbooks@gmail.com and we will send you a **FREE BOOK** in **PDF** as a **GIFT!****

Hope to see you in our future books and good luck in your drawing experience!

** in the e-mail subject please mention the name of the book you reviewed and the author.

www.ingramcontent.com/pod-product-compliance
Lightning Source LLC
Chambersburg PA
CBHW080259180526
45167CB00006B/2596